Winning TOEFL

PAGODA LANGUAGE EDUCATION CENTER

Reading Step 3

Step 1
Step 2
Step 3

Wit & Wisdom

Wit&Wisdom is the professional language publishing company of the PAGODA Education Group.

Copyright © 2024 by PAGODA Books

All rights reserved. No part of this publication may be reproduced, stored in a retrieval system, or transmitted, in any form, or by any means, electronic, mechanical, photocopying, recording or otherwise, without the prior written permission of the copyright holder and the publisher.

Published by PAGODA Books
PAGODA Books is the professional language publishing company of the PAGODA Education Group.
19F, PAGODA Tower, 419, Gangnam-daero,
Seocho-gu, Seoul, 06614, Rep. of KOREA
www.pagodabook.com

First published 2009
Fifteenth impression 2024
Printed in the Republic of Korea

ISBN 978-89-6281-059-2 (13740)

Publisher | Kyung-Sil Park
Writer | PAGODA Language Education Center

A defective book may be exchanged at the store where you purchased it.

Winning TOEFL

Reading Step 3

WINNING TOEFL READING

Introduction to iBT TOEFL

iBT TOEFL (internet-based TOEFL) is designed to measure how well non-native speakers of English read, listen, speak and write in English. The test has four sections: reading, listening, speaking, and writing. Each section of the test is worth 30 points and the highest possible score on the iBT is 120 points (30 points x 4 sections). Most questions are worth 1 point each, but some of the questions in each section are worth more than 2 points.

 → For more information, visit the ETS website (www.ets.org).

Reading Section

(1) About the passages

In the reading section, test takers will be asked to read 3 or 5 passages. Each passage consists of 600~700 words. The test time differs according to the number of the passages given.

Number of Passages	Part & Passages			Test Time
3	Part I 1 Passage	Part II 2 Passages		60 min
5	Part I 1 Passage	Part II 2 Passages	Part III 2 Passages	100 min

The passage types are:
- Exposition: a type of writing that gives information about a topic
- Argumentation: a type of writing that develops a topic in a persuasive or logical way
- Narrative: a type of writing that describes a historical or biographical event

(2) About the questions

Each passage includes 12~14 questions. The questions test student's ability in the following areas:
- Basic comprehension: understanding vocabulary, pronoun usage, identifying true or false information
- Reading to Learn: recognizing sentence structure, summarizing
- Inferencing: implying, recognizing the writer's purpose

To test these areas, 10 question types are used in the iBT TOEFL reading section.

Question Type	Explanation	Number of Questions	Related Unit
Basic Comprehension			
Vocabulary	Choose the word that is closest in meaning to the word that appears in the passage.	4~5	Unit 1
Pronoun	Identify the word to which a pronoun is referring.	0~1	Unit 1
True Information	Choose a sentence that is true according to the passage.	2~4	Unit 2
False Information	Choose a sentence that is NOT provided or NOT true according to the passage.	1	Unit 2
Sentence Simplification	Choose a sentence which is closest in meaning to the sentence that appears in the context.	1	Unit 3
Inferencing			
Inference	Draw an inference from the passage by choosing an answer that is not actually stated in the passage but is implied or can be inferred.	0~1	Unit 4
Rhetorical Purpose	Identify why the author has mentioned something in a certain way.	2	Unit 5
Insert text	Insert a sentence into the most appropriate place in the passage.	1	Unit 6
Reading to Learn			
Categorization	Categorize related information from the passage.	0~1	Unit 7
Summary	Choose the sentences that best summarize the entire passage.	0~1	Unit 8
Total		12~14	Actual Test

Winning TOEFL Reading Series

This is the third reading book in the *Winning TOEFL* series. It has eight units and each unit includes four passages. This book is for the students who are at the beginner level, so the passages are shorter (280 words on average) and easier than the original passages seen on the actual TOEFL.

Each unit consists of:

Introduction ➔ Practice 1, 2 ➔ Test 1, 2

Each section has the following subsections.

Introduction

(1) Search! Search!

Students are encouraged to find some information about the topics on the cover page of each unit using the Internet. This part will give students the opportunity to become familiar with the topics before they actually read the passages in the Practice and Test sections of each unit.

(2) Target iBT TOEFL questions

This part introduces one or two of the iBT TOEFL question types. Each unit focuses on the following iBT TOEFL question types:

Unit 1	Vocabulary Questions Pronoun Questions
Unit 2	Finding True Information Questions Finding False information Questions
Unit 3	Sentence Simplification Questions
Unit 4	Inference Questions
Unit 5	Rhetorical Purpose Questions
Unit 6	Insert Text Questions
Unit 7	Categorization Questions
Unit 8	Summary Questions

The question types introduced in this part will be practiced repetitively in the following subsections of each unit.

Practice 1, 2

(1) Warm Up
This part functions as a pre-reading activity. Students are required to reflect on their prior knowledge of the topic by answering the questions. They are also asked to guess what the passage is about using the words on the list. This section will help students practice essential pre-reading skills such as *skimming* and *scanning*.

(2) Read the passage
This section provides a passage (about 280 words) for reading. Students are encouraged to reduce their reading time by keeping track of it.

(3) Target iBT TOEFL Questions
In this part, students can practice the target question types that they were introduced to at the beginning of each unit.

(4) iBT TOEFL Vocabulary
This section lists essential expressions that appear in the reading passage. Students are asked to match the target words with their correct meanings.

(5) Wrap Up
In this section, students can review the expressions introduced in the iBT TOEFL Vocabulary section. This section also provides a summary (note) of the passage of each practice. Students can check their overall understanding of the passage by figuring out the main ideas and the organization of the passage.

Test 1, 2

This section introduces two passages that include various kinds of iBT TOEFL questions. Students can check their comprehension with these questions.

Following Unit 8, an actual test is provided.

Actual Test

Five passages are provided as an actual test. Students will be able to check their overall understanding of many iBT TOEFL questions that they were introduced to in the previous units. The test passages contain more expressions and are slightly more difficult than the passages in each unit.

WINNING TOEFL READING

Contents

- **Introduction** to iBT TOEFL — 4
- **Winning TOEFL Reading** Series — 6

Unit 1	Education	10
Unit 2	History	26
Unit 3	Biology	42
Unit 4	Environment	58
Unit 5	Political Science	74
Unit 6	Arts	90
Unit 7	Earth Science	106
Unit 8	Human Body & Nutrition	122

- **Actual Test** — 138

Passage 1	Pluto	140
Passage 2	History of the Guitar	144
Passage 3	Private vs. Public Schools	147
Passage 4	Right and Left Brain Hemisphere	150
Passage 5	The Presidential and Parliamentary Systems	153

- **Answer Keys**

UNIT 01
Education

•• Search! Search!

Find out about the topics using the Internet.

<u>Multiple Intelligences</u>, **History of the US Public School System, Anne Sullivan, Summerhill School**

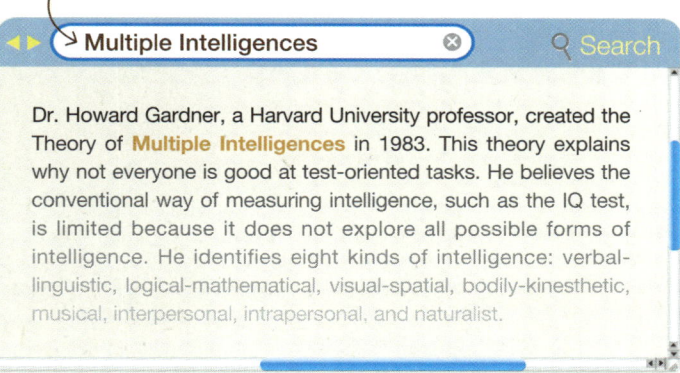

•• Target iBT TOEFL Questions

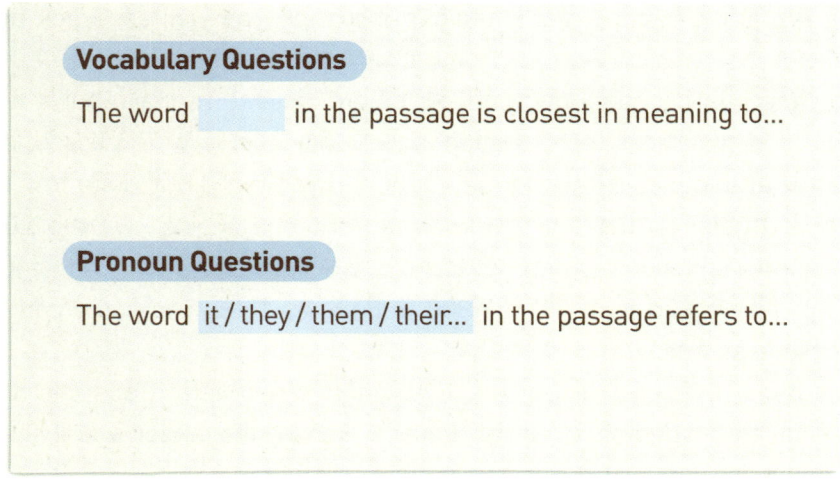

Practice 1

Warm Up

1 Do you know when the public school system began in your country?

2 Do you prefer studying in a private school or a public school?

Read the Passage

History of the US Public School System

The 3rd president of US, Thomas Jefferson, was the first person in America who suggested developing a public school system. He declared that it would become an essential part to America's continued advancement as a nation. He also concluded that it would give the American people the chance to fulfill their natural talents. His ideas were the basis for America's current education system.

Jefferson divided public education into three main divisions: primary school, intermediate school and university. Primary schools' main purpose was to teach reading, writing and basic math to all children. In intermediate schools, students were taught grammar, history, mathematics, philosophy as well as Greek and Latin.

There were publicly supported schools before Jefferson's trials, but it was not until 1852 that mandatory school attendance requirements were passed into law. Even after attendance in elementary schools was high, but quite low for intermediate schools, as the curriculum was very challenging. By the 20th century, Jefferson's ambitions turned out to be a true success, when high school graduation rates increased from 6% in 1900 to 80% by 1996. The same can be said about college as well.

It took over 150 years to get most Americans enrolled in schools, but Jefferson can be credited for its eventual success. He was the person who helped the United States develop such a dynamic education system.

* eventual: final, happening at the end

Target iBT TOEFL Questions

1 The word `essential` in the passage is closest in meaning to
- Ⓐ necessary
- Ⓑ helpful
- Ⓒ main

2 The word `advancement` in the passage is closest in meaning to
- Ⓐ exploration
- Ⓑ success
- Ⓒ improvement

3 The word `it` in the passage refers to
- Ⓐ education
- Ⓑ public school system
- Ⓒ nation

4 The word `challenging` in the passage is closest in meaning to
- Ⓐ complicated
- Ⓑ difficult
- Ⓒ useful

iBT TOEFL Vocabulary

Fill in the blanks with the appropriate words.

#			
1	_____	n	strong desire for success
2	_____	v	to carry out
3	_____	adj	essential, necessary
4	_____	v	to take a course, to attend
5	_____	n	the first step of a series of actions

- trial
- enroll
- fulfill
- mandatory
- ambition

Education •• 13

Wrap Up

A Complete the sentences with the appropriate words.

- enrolled
- ambition
- trials
- mandatory
- fulfill

1 There are _____ courses for each certification.

2 The company is filled with people who have a/an _____ to be a professional.

3 More than 20 students have _____ in the course this year.

4 After several _____, the scientists eventually made their most important discovery.

5 All participants will be able to _____ their expectations of their roles.

B Check (✔) whether the sentences are True (T) or False (F) according to the passage <History of the US Public School System>.

1 Thomas Jefferson suggested developing a private school system for the first time in the US.   T ☐   F ☐

2 Thomas Jefferson thought education could help the nation develop.   T ☐   F ☐

3 There were three main divisions in the public school systems.   T ☐   F ☐

4 Students learned reading, writing, and basic math in intermediate schools.   T ☐   F ☐

5 High school graduation rates increased from 8% in 1900 to 80% by 1996.   T ☐   F ☐

Practice 2

Warm Up

1 Which teacher were you impressed by the most and why?
2 Discuss two qualities that make a good teacher.

Read the Passage

Your time (1st): _____ min, (2nd): _____ min

Anne Sullivan

Anne Sullivan was born to poor Irish immigrant parents in Massachusetts in 1866. She had a rare eye disease, which left her blind at age ten. She spent most of her childhood undergoing many operations to restore her eyesight.

When she was 14, she enrolled in the Perkins School for the Blind. Shortly after starting her studies, she underwent an operation that partially restored her eyesight. In 1887, one year after graduating at the top of her class, she had most of her vision restored after another operation.

Interestingly, it was not Anne's personal struggles that brought her fame. Instead, it was her efforts as a teacher. Anne became a private teacher of Helen Keller, a six-year-old girl who was deaf, mute, and blind. She taught Helen to use sign language by signing into the palm of her hand. She helped Helen master reading Braille. She even taught Helen how to speak. This thorough education enabled Helen to attend some of America's most prestigious academic institutions, including the famous Radcliffe College.

The women's relationship did not, however, draw to a close after Helen's educational success. Instead, it deepened. The women lived together and continued their journey by serving as lecturers in order to raise money for the American Foundation for the Blind. It was not until Anne's death in 1936 that she and Helen parted ways. Nevertheless, Anne Sullivan's legacy as a pioneer of blind education lives on.

* immigrant: a person who leaves their home country to settle in another country
* Braille: a system of printing for blind people

Target iBT TOEFL Questions

1 The word struggles in the passage is closest in meaning to
 Ⓐ ideas   Ⓑ attempts   Ⓒ impacts

2 The word thorough in the passage is closest in meaning to
 Ⓐ unique   Ⓑ basic   Ⓒ complete

3 The word prestigious in the passage is closest in meaning to
 Ⓐ respected   Ⓑ productive   Ⓒ impressive

4 The word it in the passage refers to
 Ⓐ relationship   Ⓑ success   Ⓒ journey

iBT TOEFL Vocabulary

Fill in the blanks with the appropriate words.

1	**v**	to pass through, to experience
2	**n**	a person who finds a new way of doing something
3	**v**	to learn completely
4	**adv**	partly, not fully
5	**v**	to recover to a normal condition
6	**n**	something that someone has achieved and continues to exist

- partially
- undergo
- restore
- legacy
- pioneer
- master

Wrap Up

A Complete the sentences with the appropriate words.

- partially
- legacy
- underwent
- pioneer
- restored
- master

1 The movie is _____ based on the literature.

2 The artist is considered as a/an _____ in video art.

3 The patient _____ therapy for several months.

4 The new school program will help students _____ English.

5 Bad eyesight can be _____ by surgery.

6 Pablo Picasso left a _____ that influences modern painting.

B Complete the summary of the passage <Anne Sullivan>.

Anne Sullivan is well-known as _____ Keller's teacher. Anne was born in Massachusetts in 1866. She became blind at 10 because of a rare _____ disease, but after several _____, most of her vision was _____. She enrolled in the Perkins School for the Blind at the age of _____ and she graduated at the top of her class in 1886. After graduation, Anne began teaching Helen when Helen was _____ years old. She helped Helen learn to communicate and study further. Thanks to Anne's efforts, Helen could achieve academic success in her college. Anne and Helen continued their relationships until Anne died. Anne is considered to be a pioneer of _____ education.

Multiple Intelligences

Dr. Howard Gardner, a Harvard University professor, created the Theory of Multiple Intelligences in 1983. This theory explains why not everyone is good at test-oriented tasks. He believes the conventional way of measuring intelligence, such as the IQ test, is limited because it does not explore all possible forms of intelligence. He identifies eight kinds of intelligence: verbal-linguistic, logical-mathematical, visual-spatial, bodily-kinesthetic, musical, interpersonal, intrapersonal, and naturalist.

Unfortunately, education systems are not designed to nurture all the different kinds of intelligence. They mainly educate in a way that benefits students with verbal-linguistic or logical-mathematical intelligence, through examinations and essay writing. But what about those who are great at art and design, music, sports, interacting with others, or understanding the human mind?

Thankfully, Gardner's innovative research promotes diverse teaching methods. It inspires teachers to actively use group projects, field trips, and art activities as part of their curriculum. His theory can also help adults figure out which career they should pursue. He believes that if adults can determine their intelligence type, they will be able to choose a career that best suits them.

[■A] Regardless of age or gender, people have different skills and areas of greatness. [■B] Gardner's theory can be valuable for those who want to achieve their full potential and live a fulfilling life. [■C] The sooner society utilizes the knowledge Gardner has offered, the healthier and more productive it will be. [■D]

1 The word conventional in the passage is closest in meaning to

Ⓐ current Ⓑ correct Ⓒ traditional Ⓓ global

2 According to paragraph 1, which of the following is NOT true of the Theory of Multiple Intelligences?

Ⓐ Dr. Howard Gardner is the founder of the theory.
Ⓑ It explains how the IQ test can measure all forms of intelligence.
Ⓒ According to the theory, there are eight different types of intelligences.
Ⓓ It is a new way of measuring intelligence.

3 Which of the following best expresses the essential information in the highlighted sentence? Incorrect answer choices change the meaning in important ways or leave out essential information.

Unfortunately, education systems are not designed to nurture all the different kinds of intelligence.

Ⓐ Unluckily, teachers are not able to teach students who have different intelligences in many different ways.
Ⓑ Unfortunately, education systems have limitations in teaching students with different intelligences.
Ⓒ Unfortunately, current education systems cannot deal with students of high intelligences.
Ⓓ Unluckily, students of various intelligences are not able to design education systems.

4 The word those in the passage refers to

Ⓐ students   Ⓑ intelligences   Ⓒ Gardner   Ⓓ teachers

5 The word diverse in the passage is closest in meaning to

Ⓐ efficient   Ⓑ changeable   Ⓒ interesting   Ⓓ various

6 The word pursue in the passage is closest in meaning to

Ⓐ observe   Ⓑ take   Ⓒ ignore   Ⓓ follow

7 Look at the four squares [■] that indicate where the following sentence could be added to the passage.

Slowly, society is beginning to understand the importance of Multiple Intelligences.

Where would the sentence best fit?

8 **Directions**: An introductory sentence for a brief summary of the passage is provided below. Complete the summary by selecting THREE answer choices that express important ideas in the passage. Some sentences do not belong in the summary because they express ideas that are not presented in the passage or are minor ideas in the passage.

The Theory of Multiple Intelligences is a new way of seeing human intelligence.

-
-
-

Answer Choices

Ⓐ The theory began with Dr. Howard Gardner in 1983.

Ⓑ The theory helps students become more productive and healthier.

Ⓒ The theory can help not only children but also adults by giving them chances to understand their areas of strengths.

Ⓓ The theory categorizes human intelligences into many categories including IQ.

Ⓔ The theory inspires many teachers to utilize diverse teaching methods.

Ⓕ The theory explains why some people have high intelligence.

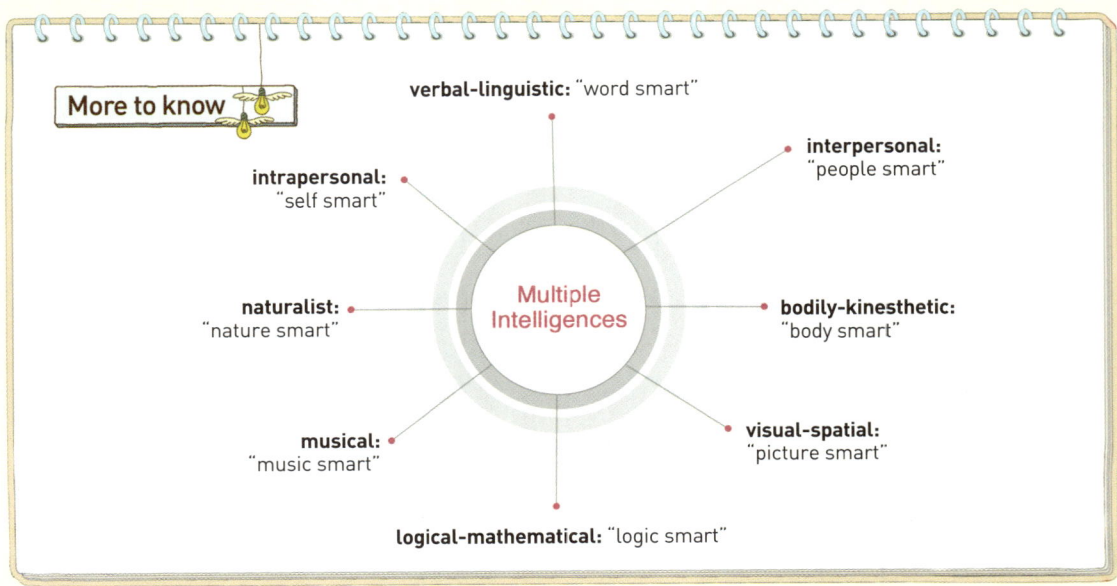

Summerhill School

Summerhill School, located in Suffolk, England, was established in 1921 by author and philosopher A.S. Neill. Summerhill, an independent school, has become the standard for progressive education. The school was founded upon the principle that education should be adjusted to each child's interests and needs.

Furthermore, Summerhill operates as a democratic community where teachers, staff and students all have an equal say in the changes that occur at the school. Whether it is a meeting about new activities, changing school rules or recent school conflicts, everyone has the chance to participate in the process. Neill believed that this can help children build a strong sense of belonging and responsibility within a community.

Summerhill offers small class sizes and an intimate atmosphere where students are given the freedom to plan their own class schedules and extra-curricular activities. Neill believed that all children should have the opportunity to lead their lives free of their teachers' preferences. Additionally, for students who fall above or below the classroom average, one-on-one classes are created. This sort of flexibility and customized environment allows the children to develop their individual talents and skills freely, both in and out of the classroom.

[■A] Summerhill has caused a stir with the British government for many years. [■B] Nevertheless, independent schools are growing in popularity among the public. [■C] After all, if A.S. Neill is right, progressive schools are the key to ensuring children's future success and happiness. [■D]

* democratic: based on the idea of social equality
* customized: made suitable

1 The word founded in the passage is closest in meaning to

Ⓐ depended   Ⓑ established   Ⓒ directed   Ⓓ extended

2 According to paragraph 2, Summerhill is considered a democratic community because

Ⓐ students decide the school policy
Ⓑ students, teachers and staff have the same right to give their opinion
Ⓒ students have the freedom to plan their class schedules
Ⓓ students do not need to take tests

3 The word it in the passage refers to

Ⓐ Summerhill   Ⓑ school   Ⓒ meeting   Ⓓ process

4 The word offers in the passage is closest in meaning to

Ⓐ provides   Ⓑ creates   Ⓒ spreads   Ⓓ has

5 The word intimate in the passage is closest in meaning to

Ⓐ odd   Ⓑ powerful   Ⓒ reliable   Ⓓ friendly

6 Which of the following best expresses the essential information in the highlighted sentence? Incorrect answer choices change the meaning in important ways or leave out essential information.

Additionally, for students who fall above or below the classroom average, one-on-one classes are created.

Ⓐ In addition, individual classes are offered for those who scored average in the class.
Ⓑ Moreover, special classes are provided to the students who want extra hours to study to get higher scores.
Ⓒ Additionally, students who scored lower or higher than the average are asked to take extra classes.
Ⓓ Different classes are also available for students who gain higher or lower scores than average.

7 Look at the four squares [■] that indicate where the following sentence could be added to the passage.

It is only a matter of time before such learning institutions become the norm.

Where would the sentence best fit?

8 According to the passage, which of the following is true of the Summerhill school?
- Ⓐ It is a public high school.
- Ⓑ Teachers change school rules through discussion.
- Ⓒ It was established by a democratic community.
- Ⓓ Students choose their own classes.

More to know   **Alexander Sutherland Neill** (October 17, 1883 - September 23, 1973)

Alexander Sutherland Neill was a progressive educator, author and founder of Summerhill school. He is best known as an advocate of freedom for children. He tried to encourage critical thinking. His ideas were originally considered controversial, but many of them are widely accepted today.

"The function of a child is to live his own life - not the life that his anxious parents think he should live, nor a life according to the purpose of the educator who thinks he knows best."

Reading Helper

A. as

Examples from the passage

- He declared that it would become an essential part to America's continued advancement **as** a nation. *(History of the US Public School System, Line 2)*

- Instead, it was her efforts **as** a teacher. *(Anne Sullivan, Line 9)*

- The women lived together and continued their journey by serving **as** lecturers in order to raise money for the American Foundation for the Blind. *(Anne Sullivan, Line 16)*

- Nevertheless, Anne Sullivan's legacy **as** a pioneer of blind education lives on. *(Anne Sullivan, Line 19)*

Complete the sentences using the appropriate expressions with *as*.

- a politician
- a world-class healthcare center
- an inventor

1 The hospital has developed _____.

2 Although Mahatma Gandhi was the leader of India during the Indian Independence Movement, he never regarded himself _____.

3 Thomas Edison's contribution _____ was what made him famous.

B. The more ... the more

Examples from the passage

- **The sooner** society utilizes the knowledge Gardner has offered, **the healthier** and **more** productive it will be.
(Multiple Intelligences, Line 20)

Complete the sentences by changing the form of the given word appropriately.

1 The more we know about each other, _____ we will perform in the contest.
(good)

2 _____ technology changes, the more it affects our daily lives.
(fast)

3 _____ the process becomes, _____ the
(clear) (high)
possibility to achieve good results is.

UNIT 02
History

•• Search! Search!

Find out about the topics using the Internet.

Stonehenge, Christopher Columbus, The Great Depression, The Silk Road

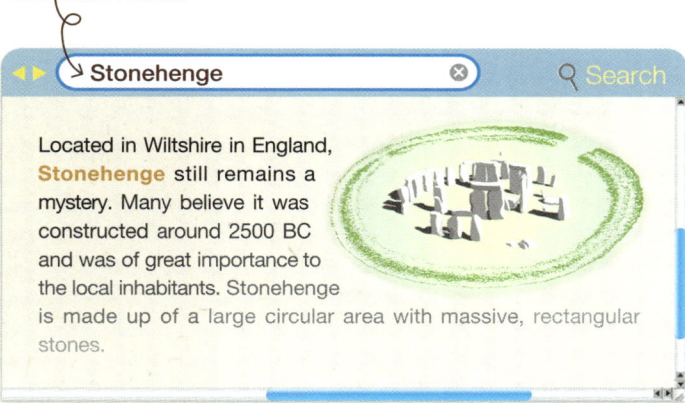

•• Target iBT TOEFL Questions

Finding true information Questions

- According to paragraph X, which of the following is true of ...?
- According to paragraph X, A did B because ...
- According to paragraph X, A is(are) ...

Finding false information Questions

- According to paragraph X, which of the following is NOT true of ...?
- All of the following are mentioned EXCEPT ...

Practice 1

Warm Up

1 Go through the passage quickly to find these words. Use what you know about these words to guess the topic.

- Columbus
- explorer
- sailing
- reached
- the Americas

Read the Passage

Your time (1st): ____ min, (2nd): ____ min

Christopher Columbus

Christopher Columbus was a famous explorer from Italy. As a child he rarely attended school but managed to teach himself Latin. He learned Latin so that he could read maps and geography books. At a young age, he was invited on a voyage through the Aegean Sea. This trip inspired him to continue exploring the planet.

Since he knew sailing to India via the route South of Africa was extremely dangerous, he wanted to discover a new path. He knew that the easier he could acquire silk and spices, the more wealth and fame he would gain. He believed that if he sailed west, he would eventually reach India. To prove this, Columbus needed a great deal of money. The Italian royals thought his request was silly. Seven years later, he finally convinced the queen of Spain, a country hungry for power and prestige after a long civil war, to sponsor his sea crossing expedition.

By August 1492, Columbus had everything he needed, including three ships. After several hardships, Columbus's ships reached a couple of islands in the Caribbean. Convinced that he had reached India, he referred to the native inhabitants as Indians, and before returning to Spain, he left a great deal of his men behind to dig for gold. In his lifetime, he made three more voyages to the Americas, but never once realized that he was not in India or of the importance of his discovery.

Target iBT TOEFL Questions

1. According to paragraph 1, Christopher Columbus learned Latin by himself in order to
   - Ⓐ teach other children
   - Ⓑ not go to school
   - Ⓒ read maps and geography books

2. According to paragraph 2, why did Columbus need money?
   - Ⓐ To convince the Italian royals
   - Ⓑ To gain wealth and fame
   - Ⓒ To sail to India

3. According to paragraph 3, what Columbus truly found was
   - Ⓐ the Americas
   - Ⓑ Spain
   - Ⓒ India

iBT TOEFL Vocabulary

Fill in the blanks with the appropriate words.

#		Definition
1	_____	n a journey on water
2	_____	n an act of asking for something
3	_____	v to arrive at
4	_____	v to persuade someone to do something
5	_____	n someone who lives in a place
6	_____	n fame, reputation that comes from success

- request
- convince
- prestige
- voyage
- reach
- inhabitant

Wrap Up

A Complete the sentences with the appropriate words.

- reached
- prestige
- convince
- voyage
- inhabitants
- request

1. Gulliver finally _____ a small, unknown island.

2. Words can be borrowed from a language that has _____.

3. The number of _____ in the Netherlands has decreased.

4. The first _____ to America by Christopher Columbus took place in 1492.

5. The _____ for the reexamination can be denied.

6. The school tried to _____ their students to support the campaign against pollution.

B Check (✔) whether the sentences are true (T) or false (F) according to the passage <Christopher Columbus>.

1. Christopher Columbus was from India.   T ☐   F ☐

2. The queen of Spain supported Columbus financially.   T ☐   F ☐

3. Columbus arrived to India in August, 1492.   T ☐   F ☐

4. Columbus's voyage through the Aegean Sea encouraged him to keep exploring the world.   T ☐   F ☐

5. Columbus wanted to find a new route because the original one took a lot of time.   T ☐   F ☐

Practice 2

Warm Up

1 Go through the passage quickly. What do you think the passage is mainly about?

☐ The construction of the Stonehenge ☐ The purposes of the Stonehenge

Read the Passage

Your time (1st): ____ min, (2nd): ____ min

Stonehenge

Located in Wiltshire in England, Stonehenge still remains a mystery. Many believe it was constructed around 2500 BC and was of great importance to the local inhabitants. Stonehenge is made up of a large circular area with massive, rectangular stones.

Studies show that the Stonehenge we know today hardly resembles the original site. One reason is that over time the inhabitants of the surrounding areas used the stones for construction. Another is a lack of respect from tourists. However, the most obvious is <u>wear and tear</u> from the weather over thousands of years.

Building the outer and inner circle of the Stonehenge was no easy task. It began as a large hill with a henge surrounding it. The henge was made and detailed with tools. By 2000 BC, the inner circle, which consists of bluestones, was made. The remarkable thing is that these bluestones weighed as much as 4 tons and were brought from mountains nearly 400 kilometers away from the actual site. How these stones were transported still remains unknown.

Archaeologists and historians are still uncertain about Stonehenge's purpose. One theory is that it was a place of worship for ancient gods or a burial site for the elite citizens of the area from prehistoric times. The possibility of it being a <u>space observatory</u> has also been considered. The last <u>plausible</u> theory is that it was a healing center. Regardless of its actual purpose and its worn state, Stonehenge remains one of the world's most valued prehistoric ruins.

* **wear and tear:** worsening of original condition due to continued use
* **space observatory:** a location used for observing stars and planets
* **plausible:** seemingly reasonable, possible

Target iBT TOEFL Questions

1. According to paragraph 3, which of the following is true of the construction of the Stonehenge?

    Ⓐ It was not easy because of a large hill.
    Ⓑ It took 2,000 years to complete.
    Ⓒ The inner circle used bluestones.

2. According to paragraph 4, all of the following are mentioned as a possible usage of the Stonehenge EXCEPT

    Ⓐ a weather observatory
    Ⓑ a burial site
    Ⓒ a healing center

iBT TOEFL Vocabulary

Fill in the blanks with the appropriate words.

#	Word		Definition
1		adj	large, big
2		v	to be like something else
3		n	admiration expressed by others
4		adj	apparent
5		adj	surprising, unusual
6		v	to move something from one place to another

- resemble
- obvious
- massive
- transport
- remarkable
- respect

Wrap Up

A Complete the sentences with the appropriate words.

- resembles
- remarkable
- respect
- massive
- obvious
- transported

1 The shape of the rock _____ the head of dragon.

2 Air pollutants were _____ by winds.

3 The medicine can take 3 days to show _____ results.

4 The process created a _____ amount of waste and became a huge problem.

5 It is vital to show _____ for different cultures.

6 Everyone will remember the professor's _____ life.

B Complete the summary note of the passage <Stonehenge>.

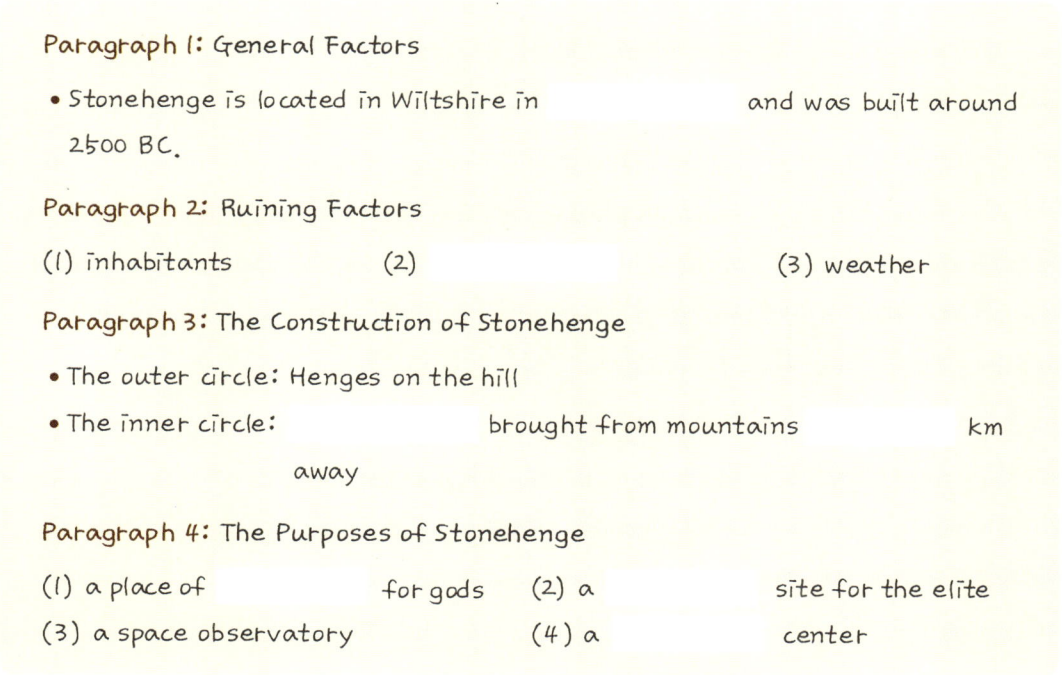

Paragraph 1: General Factors
- Stonehenge is located in Wiltshire in _____ and was built around 2500 BC.

Paragraph 2: Ruining Factors
(1) inhabitants   (2) _____   (3) weather

Paragraph 3: The Construction of Stonehenge
- The outer circle: Henges on the hill
- The inner circle: _____ brought from mountains _____ km away

Paragraph 4: The Purposes of Stonehenge
(1) a place of _____ for gods   (2) a _____ site for the elite
(3) a space observatory   (4) a _____ center

Test 1

The Great Depression

The Great Depression is known as the most desperate time in American history. It was a time of unemployment, failing banks, business closures, homelessness, and often starvation and disease. The sudden crash of the stock market caused a severe downturn in the lives of successful Americans everywhere.

The stock market's crash in October 1929 is still referred to as 'Black Tuesday.' High consumer debt, barely controlled markets, poor choices made by both banks and investors, and the increasing financial inequality between the different social classes were largely responsible. As a response to the crash, the government changed its practices. Unfortunately, these practices had negative effects on foreign economies and many began to suffer. This period is referred to as the Great Depression of the 1930's.

Immediately after the stock market collapsed, governments restricted imports or taxed them heavily. This forced citizens to purchase products made within their country. The government also gave out food because there were 13 million people who became unemployed. Millions lost farms, and the homeless rate jumped to two million.

[■A] Several developments during the 1930s allowed the economy to recover from the depression. [■B] Under Roosevelt's leadership, the US government launched New Deal programs, which offered jobs to millions of Americans and eased pressure on the economy. [■C] Additionally, Hitler's rise to power in Germany in 1933 and the Japanese invasion of China in 1937 prompted growth around the world as various countries' production of war materials increased, offering jobs to their citizens. [■D]

* debt: money owed by one person to another

1 Which of the following best expresses the essential information in the highlighted sentence? Incorrect answer choices change the meaning in important ways or leave out essential information.

<mark>The sudden crash of the stock market caused a severe downturn in the lives of successful Americans everywhere.</mark>

Ⓐ Successful Americans experienced a downturn caused by the crash of the economy.
Ⓑ Many Americans were upset because the stock market crashed suddenly.
Ⓒ The stock market crashed suddenly causing many Americans to become homeless.
Ⓓ The lives of Americans changed due to the crash of the stock market.

2 In paragraph 2, why does the author mention <mark>Black Tuesday</mark>?

Ⓐ To emphasize when the Great Depression happened
Ⓑ To show how desperate the period was
Ⓒ To explain how the government tried to solve the economic problems since then
Ⓓ To introduce one of the causes of the Great Depression

3 The word <mark>barely</mark> in the passage is closest in meaning to

Ⓐ almost
Ⓑ seldom
Ⓒ essentially
Ⓓ finally

4 In paragraph 2, all of the following are mentioned as a responsible factor of the Great Depression EXCEPT

Ⓐ poor choices made by banks and investors
Ⓑ consumers' high debt
Ⓒ financial inequality between the social classes
Ⓓ foreign economies

5 The word <mark>them</mark> in the passage refers to

Ⓐ governments
Ⓑ imports
Ⓒ citizens
Ⓓ products

6 The word prompted in the passage is closest in meaning to

Ⓐ decreased
Ⓑ gained
Ⓒ caused
Ⓓ encouraged

7 Look at the four squares [■] that indicate where the following sentence could be added to the passage.

In the US, one important development was the election of Franklin D. Roosevelt as President in 1932.

Where would the sentence best fit?

8 According to the passage, which of the following is true of the Great Depression?

Ⓐ It continued until the government changed its practices.
Ⓑ It caused the stock market to collapse.
Ⓒ A lot of people lost their jobs during the period.
Ⓓ The homeless rate began to decrease after the Great Depression.

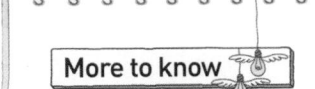

Black Tuesday

Black Tuesday was the day the New York stock market crashed (October 29, 1929). This means that the prices for stock were much higher than they were worth, and they fell sharply. Most of the people who bought high-priced stocks went bankrupt. Black Tuesday marked the beginning of the Great Depression, a period of economic crisis in the United States (1929~1939).

Test 2

The Silk Road

The Silk Road was the most famous trade route known for connecting China with India and Europe. Originally, it was only a route for trade within China, but later it was expanded by the famous Chinese traveler Chan Ch'ien. The Silk Road connected Europe with China around the time of the Roman Empire's emergence in the late third century AD.

Indians who lived near the Ganges River were instrumental in developing this international trade route. They were responsible for introducing Chinese silk, spices, and wool to the Mediterranean. Trade, however, did not only move from east to west. Ideas and information traveled across the land and bridged the two continents. The Silk Road made it possible for the Indians to introduce Buddhism to the Chinese. Additionally, Greek sculpture techniques gained popularity in China, and this eventually led to the Chinese mimicking the art by creating statues of Buddha.

[■A] It was not until nearly 500 years later in 760 AD that the Silk Road's popularity began to decrease. [■B] The main reason for this was the dangerous conditions tradesmen faced. [■C] The Silk Road had a couple of short-lived revivals in between the 11th and 12th centuries as well as the 13th and 14th centuries. [■D] Inevitably, the Silk Road's demise came with the rise in popularity of the shipping trade. Ultimately, with the Chinese government's movement toward isolating themselves from the world, the Silk Road had little hope for survival.

* **demise:** something ends
* **isolate:** to separate, to set apart

1 According to paragraph 2, all of the following were transported through the Silk Road EXCEPT

　Ⓐ statues of Buddha
　Ⓑ Greek sculpture technique
　Ⓒ silk
　Ⓓ spices

2 The word bridged in the passage is closest in meaning to

　Ⓐ linked
　Ⓑ covered
　Ⓒ stretched
　Ⓓ crossed

3 The word Additionally in the passage is closest in meaning to

　Ⓐ However
　Ⓑ Besides
　Ⓒ Instead
　Ⓓ On the other hand

4 According to paragraphs 1 and 2, which of the following was true of the Silk Road?

　Ⓐ It was the first trade route in the world.
　Ⓑ Its purpose was to connect India and Europe.
　Ⓒ It allowed trade to move from east to west.
　Ⓓ It was popular among Indian travelers.

5 According to paragraph 3, the popularity of the Silk Road decreased after several revivals because

　Ⓐ the shipping trade was dangerous for tradesmen
　Ⓑ trade by ship was more popular than trade via the Silk Road
　Ⓒ the Indian government changed the route
　Ⓓ the Chinese government developed a new route in China

6 Which of the following best expresses the essential information in the highlighted sentence in the passage? Incorrect answer choices change the meaning in important ways or leave out essential information.

> Inevitably, the Silk Road's demise came with the rise in popularity of the shipping trade.

Ⓐ As the shipping trade became less important, the Silk Road gained popularity.

Ⓑ With the development of ships, the Silk Road was no longer used.

Ⓒ The trade using the Silk Road declined as sea trade increased.

Ⓓ People avoided the shipping trade as the Silk Road became popular.

7 Look at the four squares [■] that indicate where the following sentence could be added to the passage.

Some of these dangers included severe heat in the Middle East, strong winds, animals and bandits.

Where would the sentence best fit?

More to know

Marco Polo (1254-1324)

Marco Polo is the most famous Silk Road traveler in the Western world. Although he was born in Croatia, he grew up in Venice. At that time, Venice was a center of trading and banking. Marco Polo traveled through all of China and returned to write a book. The book was translated into many different languages and is known in English as <The Travels of Marco Polo>.

Reading Helper

A. Finding the subjects and the verbs of the sentences

> **Examples from the passage**
> - <u>Christopher Columbus</u> <u>was</u> a famous explorer from Italy.
>   subject   verb   (Christopher Columbus, Line 1)
> - <u>Building the outer and inner circle of the Stonehenge</u> <u>was</u> no easy task.
>   subject   verb   (Stonehenge, Line 11)

The following are the sentences from the passages in Unit 2. Find the subject and the verb of each sentence.

1 The Italian royals thought his request was silly.

2 How these stones were transported still remains unknown.

3 The sudden crash of the stock market caused a severe downturn in the lives of successful Americans everywhere.

4 The stock market's crash in October 1929 is still referred to as 'Black Tuesday.'

5 The Silk Road was the most famous trade route known for connecting China with India and Europe.

6 Indians who lived near the Ganges River were instrumental in developing this international trade route.

7 Additionally, Greek sculpture techniques gained popularity in China, and this eventually led to the Chinese mimicking the art by creating statues of Buddha.

UNIT 03
Biology

•• Search! Search!

Find out about the topics using the Internet.
Photosynthesis, Fungi, The Social Order of Honeybees, Symbiosis

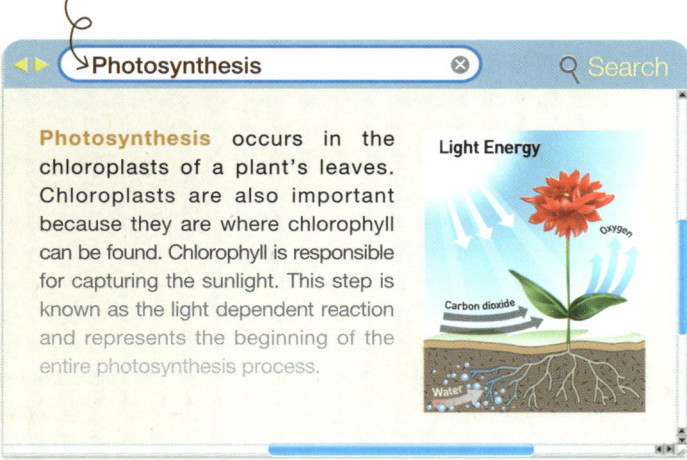

•• Target iBT TOEFL Questions

Sentence Simplification Questions

Which of the following best expresses the essential information in the highlighted sentence in the passage? Incorrect answer choices change the meaning in important ways or leave out essential information.

A sentence

Practice 1

Warm Up

1 Fungi are organisms, which are neither plants nor animals. Choose two examples that match this explanation.

- yeasts
- roses
- rabbits
- molds

Read the Passage

Your time (1st): ____ min, (2nd): ____ min

Fungi

Fungi are organisms, which are neither plants nor animals. The sizes and formations of fungi differ from one type to another. Many are easily seen with the naked eye, but others require the use of a microscope. Now, they exist in what is known as the fungal kingdom, but it took scientists quite some time to discover that fungi are extremely different from plants. The first major difference is that fungi do not have chlorophyll, which is known to give green plants their color. Additionally, fungi do not require energy from the sun to make food.

Fungi survive by feeding on living matter that is breaking down, or more simply put, dying. Many kinds of fungi play an essential role in the <u>decomposition</u> process. This brings nutrients back into the land. Fungi are also an important part of modern human life. We use fungi to make some alcoholic beverages, bread, vitamins, and cleaning supplies.

Fungi can also be used in professional medicine. Certain types of fungi can be used for antibiotics such as penicillin. More importantly, such drugs can increase the potential success rate of organ transplants within humans.

Not all fungi are helpful, though. Some act like parasites and use other organisms as food. These types of fungi often cause disease, especially in humans. The most commonly known disease is athlete's foot. However, helpful fungi may be in our daily lives, fighting such diseases.

* **decomposition:** the process of rotting or decay

Target iBT TOEFL Questions

1 Which of the following best expresses the essential information in the highlighted sentence in the passage? Incorrect answer choices change the meaning in important ways or leave out essential information.

> Fungi are organisms, which are neither plants nor animals.

Ⓐ Fungi can be categorized as both plants and animals.
Ⓑ Fungi are different from plants and animals.
Ⓒ Fungi are unique in that they are not similar to plants or animals.

2 Which of the following best expresses the essential information in the highlighted sentence in the passage? Incorrect answer choices change the meaning in important ways or leave out essential information.

> Many are easily seen with the naked eye, but others require the use of a microscope.

Ⓐ Some fungi can be seen with a microscope, but others cannot.
Ⓑ We need to use a microscope to see many fungi easily.
Ⓒ Some can be found easily with eyes, but others can be seen only under a microscope.

iBT TOEFL Vocabulary

Fill in the blanks with the appropriate words.

#		Definition
1		**n** a living thing
2		**n** the operation of moving an organ
3		**adv** in addition, besides
4		**n** chemical substances that destroy bacteria
5		**adj** possible, likely in the future

- transplant
- potential
- organism
- antibiotic
- additionally

Wrap Up

A Complete the sentences with the appropriate words.

- organism
- antibiotic
- transplant
- potential
- additionally

1. The book is very easy to read. _____, it is an inspiring book.

2. The side effects of the _____ can be serious when it is overused.

3. There might be some _____ risks in the system.

4. Body organ _____ is the moving of an organ from one body to another.

5. One of the key features of a living _____ is its interaction with its environment.

B Complete the summary note of the passage <Fungi>.

- Fungi
    organisms that are neither _____ nor animals

- Features
    (1) do not have chlorophyll
    (2) do not require energy from the _____ to make food
    (3) survive by feeding on living matter that is in the _____ process

- Beneficial Uses
    (1) _____ source (e.g. alcoholic beverages, bread, vitamins)
    (2) _____ (e.g. antibiotic)

- Harmful effects
    (1) some cause disease. (e.g. athlete's _____)

Practice 2

Warm Up

1 What materials are required for photosynthesis? Choose three.

☐ sunlight ☐ water ☐ soil ☐ CO_2 (carbon dioxide)

Read the Passage

Photosynthesis

Plants are unique from all other organisms because they are able to produce their own food. Plants use energy from the sun as well as water, carbon dioxide and chlorophyll to produce sugar glucose. This sugar glucose is stored in the leaves. This process is called photosynthesis and it has two main parts.

Photosynthesis occurs in the chloroplasts of a plant's leaves. Chloroplasts are also important because they are where chlorophyll can be found. Chlorophyll is responsible for capturing the sunlight. This step is known as the light dependent reaction and represents the beginning of the entire photosynthesis process. Once the sun's energy is stored, it gets converted into a chemical called ATP.

The second part of the process takes place when plants use ATP to create glucose. Plants combine ATP with oxygen, chlorophyll and water to produce glucose. Then, the plant uses the glucose to build more complex substances such as proteins and fats.

A byproduct of photosynthesis, essential to most living organisms, is oxygen. Plants take in carbon dioxide from the air and release oxygen, thereby making our air cleaner. This is similar to the way human lungs work. However, our lungs take in oxygen and release carbon dioxide. Because of this process, forests have earned the nickname 'the lungs of the Earth'. It is through the process of photosynthesis that we are able to understand how much plants and animals depend upon each other for survival.

* chlorophyll: a green pigment that provides green color to plants

Target iBT TOEFL Questions

1. Which of the following best expresses the essential information in the highlighted sentence in the passage? Incorrect answer choices change the meaning in important ways or leave out essential information.

   > Plants are unique from all other organisms because they are able to produce their own food.

   Ⓐ The ability to produce their own food is the special feature that plants have.
   Ⓑ Only limited numbers of plants can make their own energy through photosynthesis.
   Ⓒ Plants are special in that they are able to turn sunlight into energy for other organisms.

2. Which of the following best expresses the essential information in the highlighted sentence in the passage? Incorrect answer choices change the meaning in important ways or leave out essential information.

   > It is through the process of photosynthesis that we are able to understand how much plants and animals depend upon each other for survival.

   Ⓐ Photosynthesis helps us understand how much plants depend on animals for survival.
   Ⓑ No living organisms can live without the help from other organisms.
   Ⓒ Through photosynthesis, we can understand how much living organisms rely on each other to survive.

iBT TOEFL Vocabulary

Fill in the blanks with the appropriate words.

1. _____ ⓝ a particular procedure of an action
2. _____ ⓥ to seize
3. _____ ⓥ to replace with another
4. _____ ⓝ a secondary or an unexpected material made by the production of another material
5. _____ ⓥ to let go of

- release
- process
- byproduct
- convert
- capture

Wrap Up

A Complete the sentences with the appropriate words.

- process
- captured
- converted
- byproduct
- release

1 For the first time, the scientists _____ sound into light.

2 Some students became more social through the _____ of homeschooling.

3 Ants _____ pheromones on the ground while moving.

4 A 10-foot-long snake was _____ in the trap.

5 Carbon dioxide is a natural _____ of animal life.

B Complete the summary note of the passage <Photosynthesis>.

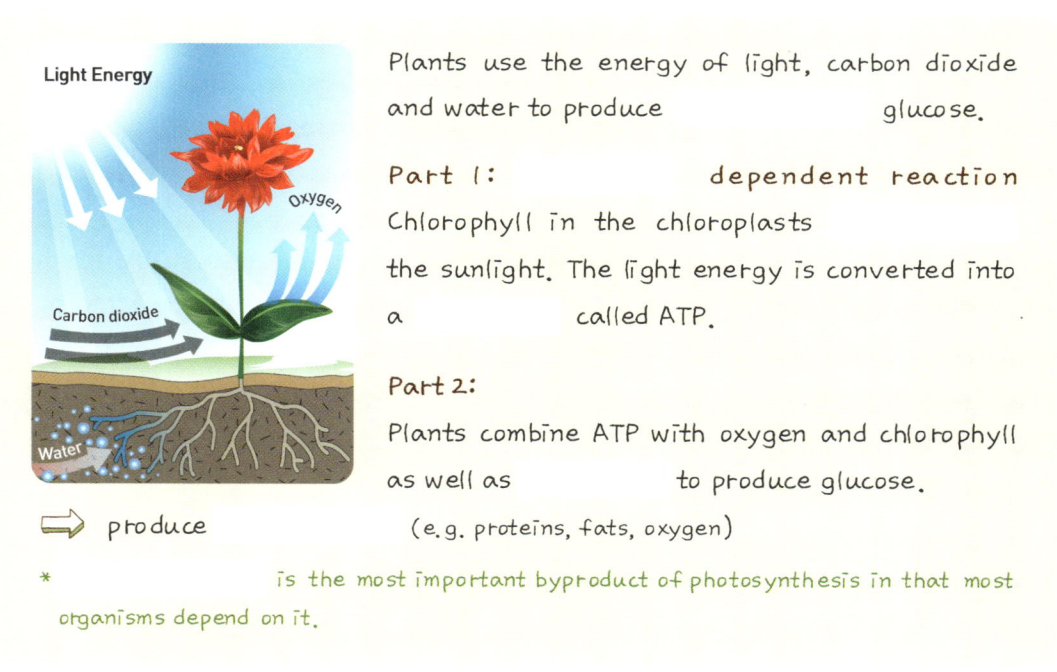

Plants use the energy of light, carbon dioxide and water to produce _____ glucose.

Part 1: _____ dependent reaction
Chlorophyll in the chloroplasts _____ the sunlight. The light energy is converted into a _____ called ATP.

Part 2:
Plants combine ATP with oxygen and chlorophyll as well as _____ to produce glucose.

⇨ produce (e.g. proteins, fats, oxygen)

* _____ is the most important byproduct of photosynthesis in that most organisms depend on it.

Test 1

The Social Order of Honeybees

Honeybees are insects that live in highly organized communities. They build and live in a nest known as a hive. Hives can house nearly 20,000 bees at the busiest of times. Bees exist in groups known as castes. There are three castes—queens, drones and workers—that represent the different jobs for which the bees will be responsible.

For every hive, there is only a single queen and her job is to reproduce. Daily she produces over 1,000 eggs and can live up to eight years. Unlike the other bees, she has a long body and is able to use her stinger many times.

The next caste of bees is known as the drones. All drones are males and they are responsible for mating with the queen bee. The major difference between them and other bees is that drones have larger eyes. Their large eyes allow them to find queen bees when flying outside the hive. This ability allows the species to thrive and continue. Another major difference is that their life spans are no longer than 8 weeks.

[■A] Worker bees are unable to reproduce and are responsible for the building and repair of the hive. [■B] They are generally broken down into two groups: house bees and field bees. [■C] The house bees not only tend to the needs of the queen and the drones but also raise the young. The bees that are a bit older, the field bees, are depended on for gathering material for hive construction and food in the form of nectar. [■D]

* **house:** to store, to contain

1. The word **highly** in the passage is closest in meaning to

   Ⓐ basically   Ⓑ rapidly   Ⓒ extremely   Ⓓ nearly

2. According to paragraph 1, which of the following is NOT true of honeybees?

   Ⓐ They live in an organized group.
   Ⓑ They have different roles.
   Ⓒ They create their own nest.
   Ⓓ They are divided into four categories.

3. Which of the following best expresses the essential information in the highlighted sentence in the passage? Incorrect answer choices change the meaning in important ways or leave out essential information.

   For every hive, there is only a single queen and her job is to reproduce.

   Ⓐ Every hive has only one queen and the queen reproduces.
   Ⓑ Only one queen among many others can reproduce in the hives.
   Ⓒ Each hive is for the queen bee's reproduction.
   Ⓓ There is a hive that has a single queen which can reproduce.

4. Which of the following best expresses the essential information in the highlighted sentence in the passage? Incorrect answer choices change the meaning in important ways or leave out essential information.

   Their large eyes allow them to find queen bees when flying outside the hive.

   Ⓐ Drones can find flying queen bees easily with their big eyes.
   Ⓑ Big eyes allow drones to see queen bees when they fly outside.
   Ⓒ With huge eyes, queen bees can see the flying drones when flying outside.
   Ⓓ Drones' large eyes can be helpful for them to find queen bees.

5. The word **thrive** in the passage is closest in meaning to

   Ⓐ survive   Ⓑ live   Ⓒ flourish   Ⓓ exist

6 The word their in the passage refers to

  Ⓐ drones   Ⓑ worker bees   Ⓒ queen bees   Ⓓ species

7 Look at the four squares [■] that indicate where the following sentence could be added to the passage.

Lastly, the other caste is the worker bees.

Where would the sentence best fit?

8 Directions: Complete the table below about the two castes of bees. Match the phrases to the appropriate category. TWO of the answer choices will NOT be used.

Answer Choices

Ⓐ have big eyes
Ⓑ can live up to eight weeks
Ⓒ are only males
Ⓓ are divided into two groups
Ⓔ produce over 1,000 eggs
Ⓕ can sting many times
Ⓖ are responsible for the construction of the hive

Drones
- _____
- _____
- _____

Worker bees
- _____
- _____

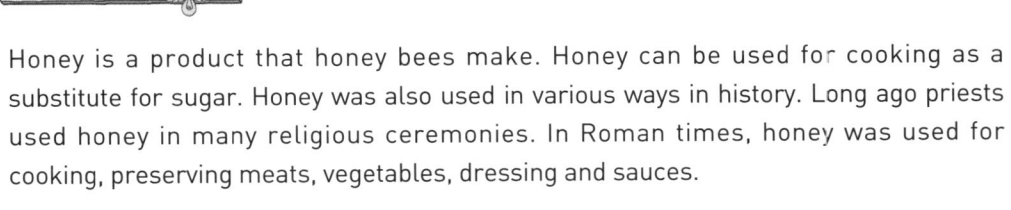

More to know **Honey**

Honey is a product that honey bees make. Honey can be used for cooking as a substitute for sugar. Honey was also used in various ways in history. Long ago priests used honey in many religious ceremonies. In Roman times, honey was used for cooking, preserving meats, vegetables, dressing and sauces.

Test 2

Symbiosis

It is a very common idea that species and creatures within each species have to compete for survival. However, competition is not always required to live. Some organisms have relationships with others in which one or both organisms benefit and become stronger. This is called symbiosis and there are three different kinds of such relationships.

One type of symbiosis, parasitism, is a relationship between two organisms, which weakens one while the other benefits or grows stronger. The organism that benefits from this relationship is called a parasite. Typically, parasites live on or in another organism, which is called the host. A common example of parasitism is between fleas and animals. The fleas live on animals' skin and suck their blood. The blood allows the flea to survive, but causes the animal pain and irritation. Parasites will never kill their hosts. They are generally smaller than them and can live on both plants and animals.

The second type of symbiotic relationships is mutualism. This is a relationship between two organisms, in which both organisms gain something. Bees and flowers are a perfect example of mutualism. Bees get their food – nectar – from flowers, but in return, they pollinate the flowers. This allows the flowers to reproduce.

[■A] The last type of symbiotic relationship is commensalism. [■B] This is when an organism benefits from the relationship and the other does not benefit, but remains unharmed. [■C] Millions of bacteria live on our skin. Without our bodies, the bacteria struggle to live. [■D] They eat the dead cells on our skin.

* cell: the basic structural unit of all living organisms

1. Which of the following best expresses the essential information in the highlighted sentence in the passage? Incorrect answer choices change the meaning in important ways or leave out essential information.

   Some organisms have relationships with others in which one or both organisms benefit and become stronger.

   Ⓐ Some organisms are related to others in a way that they benefit from the relationship.
   Ⓑ Not all organisms can benefit from their relationships with other organisms.
   Ⓒ One or both organisms always gain benefit in a relationship with others.
   Ⓓ Sometimes the relationships between organisms benefit one or both organisms.

2. The word **Typically** in the passage is closest in meaning to

   Ⓐ generally   Ⓑ gradually   Ⓒ apparently   Ⓓ totally

3. The word **them** in the passage refers to

   Ⓐ parasites   Ⓑ hosts   Ⓒ plants   Ⓓ animals

4. According to paragraph 2, which of the following is NOT true of parasitism?

   Ⓐ The organism that benefits from parasitism is called a parasite.
   Ⓑ Parasites are the organisms that live on the hosts.
   Ⓒ Fleas are an example of parasites.
   Ⓓ Parasites can kill their hosts.

5. The word **gain** in the passage is closest in meaning to

   Ⓐ get   Ⓑ lose   Ⓒ change   Ⓓ need

6. Look at the four squares [■] that indicate where the following sentence could be added to the passage.

   As humans, commensalism is a part of our daily lives, even though we may not notice.

   Where would the sentence best fit?

7 What's the function of paragraph 1 as it relates to the rest of the passage?

Ⓐ It explains how organisms compete each other for survival.
Ⓑ It provides a general introduction to symbiosis.
Ⓒ It emphasizes how species and creatures interact with each other.
Ⓓ It briefly describes three kinds of symbiosis.

8 Directions: Complete the table below about the two kinds of symbiotic relationships. Match the statements to the appropriate category. TWO of the answer choices will NOT be used.

Answer Choices

Ⓐ It is the relationship between a parasite and a host.
Ⓑ One of the two organisms that does not benefit remains unharmed.
Ⓒ The common example of this relationship is between fleas and humans.
Ⓓ The example of this relationship can be seen between bees and flowers.
Ⓔ The organism gets something from this relationship while the other does not.
Ⓕ Millions of bacteria and humans are in such a relationship.
Ⓖ Both organisms gain benefits from this relationship.

Commensalism
- _____
- _____
- _____

Mutualism
- _____
- _____

Reading Helper

A. Talking about differences ❶

> **Examples from the passage**
>
> - The sizes and formations of fungi **differ from** one type to another. (Fungi, Line 1)
>
> - Now, they exist in what is known as the fungal kingdom, but it took scientists quite some time to discover that fungi **are** extremely **different from** plants. (Fungi, Line 3)
>
> - Plants **are unique from** all other organisms because they are able to produce their own food. (Photosynthesis, Line 1)

Rewrite the sentences using the given expressions as seen in the example.

> Now, they exist in what is known as the fungal kingdom, but it took scientists quite some time to discover that fungi **are** extremely **different from** plants. (differ from)
>
> ⇨ Now, they exist in what is known as the fungal kingdom, but it took scientists quite some time to discover that fungi extremely **differ from** plants.

1 Plants **are unique from** all other organisms because they are able to produce their own food. (differ from)

2 The sizes and formations of fungi **differ from** one type to another. (be different from)

B. Talking about differences ❷

> **Examples from the passage**
>
> - **The first major difference is that** fungi do not have chlorophyll, which is known to give green plants their color.
>   (Fungi, Line 5)

Go through the passage <The Social Order of Honeybees> in Unit 3 and find the two sentences below. Complete the sentences as they appeared in the passages.

1 _____

   _____ drones have larger eyes.

2 _____

   their life spans are no longer than 8 weeks.

Biology •• 57

UNIT 04 Environment

•• Search! Search!

Find out about the topics using the Internet.
Dams, **Natural Resources, Global Warming, Yellow Dust**

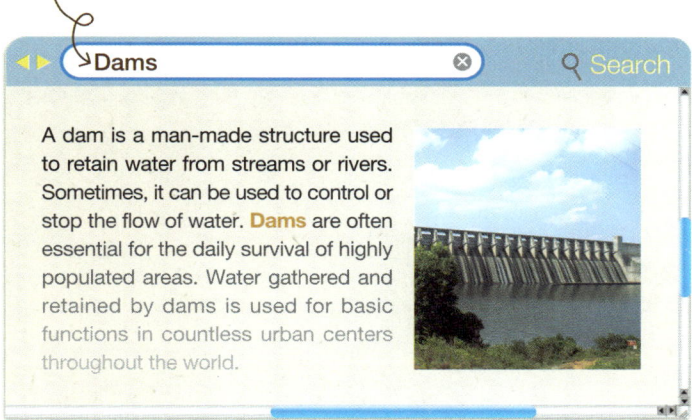

•• Target iBT TOEFL Questions

Inference Questions

- What can be inferred from paragraph X about _____?
- According to paragraph X, it can be inferred about _____ that...

Practice 1

Warm Up

1 List two more ways to protect natural resources.

- Recycle papers, cans, and plastics.
- _____
- _____

Read the Passage

Your time (1st): ____ min, (2nd): ____ min

Natural Resources

Nature has provided us with so many essential tools that we use in our daily lives, often for survival. They are called natural resources. There are many different types of natural resources, and some examples include air, oil, water, plants, animals, coal, and trees. With the world rapidly changing, and large countries such as India and China developing, natural resources are being used at an extraordinary rate.

Natural resources can be divided into two groups: renewable and non-renewable. The difference is whether the resource recovers naturally over time. Renewable resources such as animals, trees and other plants can be replaced within our lifetime. However, even though these resources are not finite, humans should still maintain a high-level of respect for the environment and use only what is absolutely necessary.

Non-renewable resources are materials and substances that can take up to a million years for nature to replace. Non-renewable resources can be traded between countries. Some of the resource rich countries in the Middle East, such as Iran and Saudi Arabia, export oil to other countries. Other non-renewable resources are coal, natural gas, and metal.

Whether it is a renewable or non-renewable resource, we must protect and use the given supplies wisely. This is called conservation. It is also better known as 'reduction' in the environment campaign of Reduce, Reuse, Recycle. Reusing items and recycling are also effective ways of protecting our natural resources.

Target iBT TOEFL Questions

1 What can be inferred from paragraph 3 about non-renewable resources?

  Ⓐ They are very expensive.
  Ⓑ They are finite.
  Ⓒ Most of them are usually used in developing countries.
  Ⓓ They produce waste materials on Earth.

2 The word rapidly in the passage is closest in meaning to

  Ⓐ constantly
  Ⓑ quickly
  Ⓒ seriously

iBT TOEFL Vocabulary

Fill in the blanks with the appropriate words.

#	Word	Definition
1		**adv** quickly, fast
2		**adj** unusual, uncommon
3		**adj** having limits
4		**v** to keep something the same as before
5		**adv** completely, without any exceptions
6		**n** something that is provided

- rapidly
- maintain
- supply
- absolutely
- extraordinary
- finite

Environment •• **61**

Wrap Up

A Complete the sentences with the appropriate words.

- supply
- extraordinary
- absolutely
- rapidly
- finite
- maintain

1 The oil prices will become higher and higher due to its limited _____.

2 The world has _____ natural resources, thus people need to use them wisely.

3 People say it is not easy to _____ balance between their work and their personal life.

4 The geologists are _____ certain that the earthquake will happen.

5 The unemployment rate has increased _____ during the last three months.

6 The _____ beginning of the novel is the key to its popularity.

B Complete the summary note of the passage <Natural Resources>.

- Natural resources
  essential to our lives (e.g. air, oil, water, plants, animals, coal, and trees)

- Two types of natural resources
  (1) _____ : can be replaced (e.g. animals, trees, other plants)
  (2) _____ : finite, cannot be replaced within our lifetime
      (e.g. oil, coal, _____ , _____)

- We must protect the given supplies wisely through "reducing, reusing, and _____."

Practice 2

Warm Up

1 The following list shows some of the purposes of the dams. Find one that is not the purpose of the dams.

- ☐ recreation
- ☐ generation of hydroelectricity
- ☐ water supply
- ☐ flood control
- ☐ protection of the ecosystem

Read the Passage

Your time (1st): _____ min, (2nd): _____ min

Dams

A dam is a man-made structure used to retain water from streams or rivers. Sometimes, it can be used to control or stop the flow of water. Dams are often essential for the daily survival of highly populated areas. Water gathered and retained by dams is used for basic functions in countless urban centers throughout the world.

However, creating a water supply for urban areas is not the sole purpose of dams. One of the most important usages is to generate power, namely hydroelectric power. The dammed water is used to create electricity. A hydroelectric source requires no fuel and is cheaper than other alternative energies, including solar, wind and nuclear power.

Dams are also essential to stabilizing water flow, which is necessary for the day-to-day functioning and productivity of farms. On farms, dams are used in irrigation systems responsible for sending and distributing the correct amount of water to crops daily.

Dams may be useful, but they also disrupt the ecology of rivers. Generally, rivers have stable temperatures throughout, but this is not true of water collected by dams. The water in dams does not have a constant temperature. The temperature of the dam water is seasonally higher than the normal temperature of the river. The water closest to the surface is far warmer than that towards the bottom. Moreover, dam construction also results in people losing their homes and being forced to relocate. This is the case for nearly 80 million people.

Target iBT TOEFL Questions

1. According to paragraph 2, what can be inferred about a hydroelectric source?

   Ⓐ It is the only way to generate alternative energy for now.
   Ⓑ It is the most cost effective way of generating energy.
   Ⓒ It is one of the most important sources in creating a water supply.

2. Based on the information in paragraph 4, what can be inferred about the dam water?

   Ⓐ It might be hard for some organisms to adapt or survive there.
   Ⓑ It does not have any water flow.
   Ⓒ The top of the water has a stable temperature.

iBT TOEFL Vocabulary

Fill in the blanks with the appropriate words.

1. _____ v to hold something within
2. _____ adj too numerous to count
3. _____ v to create, to make
4. _____ n the power to produce
5. _____ v to give out, to spread
6. _____ v to interrupt, to break in

- generate
- productivity
- retain
- countless
- disrupt
- distribute

Wrap Up

A Complete the sentences with the appropriate words.

- disrupt
- distribute
- retained
- countless
- generate
- productivity

1. The purpose of the experiment was to _____ electricity using the solar energy.

2. The company tried to _____ the workload evenly to the employees.

3. More moisture is _____ by plants leaves when there is high moisture in the air.

4. The use of the new machine has increased the _____ of the factory by 20%.

5. Dams are expensive to build and _____ the environment.

6. There can be _____ ways of lowering the environmental pollution.

B Complete the summary note of the passage <Dams>.

1. What is a dam?
   - A dam is
2. Dams are used to
   (1) control or stop the _____ of water
   (2) supply water for _____ areas
   (3) generate
   (4) stabilize water flow: water for irrigation
3. Disadvantages of dams
   - Dams may _____ the ecology of rivers. The _____ of dams also results in people leaving their homes.

Test 1

Global Warming

The average temperatures on Earth have risen significantly over the last century. This process is called global warming. It is caused by the release of greenhouse gases such as carbon dioxide, methane, and ozone into the atmosphere. Carbon dioxide causes the most damage by behaving as a blanket, which traps hot air and causes the Earth to warm.

With numerous countries developing rapidly, the release of greenhouse gases into the atmosphere continues to increase. All of this industrialization burns a great deal of fossil fuels such as oil, and releases extraordinary amounts of carbon dioxide. Furthermore, deforestation reverses the positive effects that trees have on the homeostasis of life on Earth.

These rising temperatures on Earth have many negative effects. The heating of the planet is causing polar and glacial ice to melt. The more ice melts, the more it expands and sea levels rise. This will result in the eventual flooding of many important coastal areas, leaving many urban centers destroyed. Experts believe that global warming is also responsible for the noticeably high frequency and intensity of hurricanes, heat waves and other extreme weather conditions. [■A]

[■B] Such extreme changes in weather can damage many animal habitats. [■C] Global warming cannot be stopped completely, but we can slow it down by conserving our resources and relying on eco-friendly energy sources such as wind, water and solar power to support our daily needs. [■D]

1. The word significantly in the passage is closest in meaning to
   Ⓐ widely   Ⓑ sharply   Ⓒ greatly   Ⓓ rapidly

2. The word numerous in the passage is closest in meaning to
   Ⓐ large   Ⓑ many   Ⓒ great   Ⓓ general

3 What can be inferred from paragraph 2 about carbon dioxide?

Ⓐ Trees remove carbon dioxide from the atmosphere.
Ⓑ Carbon dioxide is not released in developed countries.
Ⓒ Forests are destroyed due to the release of carbon dioxide.
Ⓓ Carbon dioxide is likely to be released more in rural areas than in urban areas.

4 The word it in the passage refers to

Ⓐ the Earth   Ⓑ heating   Ⓒ planet   Ⓓ ice

5 According to paragraph 3, which of the following is NOT mentioned as a result of rising temperatures?

Ⓐ It causes land levels to rise.
Ⓑ It causes ice to melt.
Ⓒ It causes more hurricanes than normal.
Ⓓ It changes weather conditions.

6 Look at the four squares [■] that indicate where the following sentence could be added to the passage.

They can also reduce crop productivity and even lead to the extinction of countless animal species.

Where would the sentence best fit?

7 Which of the following best expresses the essential information in the highlighted sentence in the passage? Incorrect answer choices change the meaning in important ways or leave out essential information.

Global warming cannot be stopped completely, but we can slow it down by conserving our resources and relying on eco-friendly energy sources such as wind, water and solar power to support our daily needs.

Ⓐ Although global warming will continue, it can be slowed down if we save our resources and use alternative energy sources.
Ⓑ If we use the energy sources such as wind, water, and solar power wisely, there will be no such thing like global warming.
Ⓒ Global warming is impossible to stop, but if we save our energy sources it can be delayed.
Ⓓ Eco-friendly energy sources are necessary in our daily lives to slow down global warming.

Environment • **67**

8 According to the passage, which of the following is true of carbon dioxide?

    Ⓐ It consists of greenhouse gases.
    Ⓑ It stops cold air to circulate.
    Ⓒ It lowers the temperatures of the Earth.
    Ⓓ It is responsible for deforestation.

9 Directions: An introductory sentence for a brief summary of the passage is provided below. Complete the summary by selecting THREE answer choices that express important ideas in the passage. Some sentences do not belong in the summary because they express ideas that are not presented in the passage or are minor ideas in the passage.

Global warming is the increase in the average temperature of the Earth's atmosphere.

-
-
-

Answer Choices

Ⓐ The rising temperatures can cause many problems on Earth.
Ⓑ Greenhouse gases include carbon dioxide, methane, and ozone.
Ⓒ Many countries suffer from the release of greenhouse gases into the atmosphere.
Ⓓ Industrialization is one of the reasons for the rising temperatures on Earth.
Ⓔ Global warming can be slowed down by conserving current resources and finding eco-friendly resources.
Ⓕ Using eco-friendly resources can be a solution for increasing greenhouse gases.

More to know | **Facts about Global Warming**

- Average temperatures have increased 0.8 degree Celsius around the world since 1880.
- The last two decades of the 20th century were the hottest in 400 years.
- Average temperatures in Alaska have climbed twice the global average.
- Arctic ice is quickly melting and polar bears are already suffering from the disappearing sea-ice.

Yellow Dust

Yellow dust storms are a serious problem in East Asia. Yellow dust, also known as yellow wind or Asian dust, mainly occurs each year in the spring. Yellow dust storms are clouds of small pieces of soil, sulphur, ash, bacteria, pesticides and other lethal toxins that blow from Mongolia and northern China to Korea and Japan.

With China's ever-increasing industrialization, the yellow dust problem has intensified. The World Health Organization warns of the terrible side effects of yellow dust. For instance, these storms cause severe health problems, including respiratory disorders such as asthma and lung cancer.

Yellow dust affects our lives in many other ways. Aside from making it difficult to breathe, yellow dust decreases visibility. [■A] With lower visibility, driving becomes more difficult, and so do smaller things such as playing sports or going for walks outdoors. [■B] It also ruins farms' soil quality by depositing various pollutants. [■C] In addition, these storms adversely affect wildlife by destroying some animals' habitats, especially the waters where we fish. [■D]

The good news is that Mongolia, China, Japan and South Korea are working together to soften the impact of yellow dust. They are developing a monitoring system to track the storms so that communities can be warned in advance to stay indoors. This will help people to know when they should avoid being outside and to protect themselves with face masks, hats and glasses.

* **respiratory:** relating to breathing

1 The word lethal in the passage is closest in meaning to

Ⓐ well-known   Ⓑ notorious   Ⓒ fatal   Ⓓ unique

2 The word intensified in the passage is closest in meaning to

   Ⓐ escalated　　　　Ⓑ disappeared　　　　Ⓒ occurred　　　　Ⓓ limited

3 According to paragraphs 1 and 2, which of the following is NOT true of yellow dust?

   Ⓐ It includes harmful particles that can develop health problems.
   Ⓑ It is due to pollution in Japan and Korea.
   Ⓒ It is also called yellow wind or Asian dust.
   Ⓓ The problem is getting serious due to industrialization of China.

4 The word adversely in the passage is closest in meaning to

   Ⓐ consequently　　　Ⓑ negatively　　　Ⓒ seriously　　　Ⓓ basically

5 According to paragraph 3, all of the following are mentioned as an effect of yellow dust EXCEPT problems in

   Ⓐ breathing　　　Ⓑ visibility　　　Ⓒ digestion　　　Ⓓ soil quality

6 Look at the four squares [■] that indicate where the following sentence could be added to the passage.

   By eating such fish, both humans and animals ingest those very same toxins, increasing our chances of developing health problems.

   Where would the sentence best fit?

7 According to the passage, what can be inferred about yellow dust?

   Ⓐ The phenomenon will spread rapidly around the world.
   Ⓑ It is a natural change that takes place on Earth.
   Ⓒ East Asian countries need to spend a lot of money to solve the problem.
   Ⓓ It can be reduced by lowering air pollution in China.

8 **Directions**: An introductory sentence for a brief summary of the passage is provided below. Complete the summary by selecting THREE answer choices that express important ideas in the passage. Some sentences do not belong in the summary because they express ideas that are not presented in the passage or are minor ideas in the passage.

Yellow dust storms are a seasonal phenomenon that affects East Asia during the springtime.

-
-
-

Answer Choices

Ⓐ Yellow dust causes inconveniences in our daily lives.
Ⓑ Yellow dust storms are getting worse due to China's industrialization.
Ⓒ Yellow dust storms lower visibility.
Ⓓ Yellow dust storms blow from Korea and Japan to Mongolia and northern China.
Ⓔ Many East Asian countries are trying to find ways to solve the yellow dust problems.
Ⓕ People should not go out when there is yellow dust storms.

| More to know | **What to Do during Yellow Dust Season** |

- If possible, stay inside.
- Avoid densely populated areas.
- Apply moisturizing cream to exposed skin.
- Wear protective glasses and a mask to avoid small particles.
- Wash your hands, brush your teeth, and take a bath more often than normal.

Reading Helper

A. The Usage of Adverbs ❶

> **Examples from the passage**
>
> - The difference is whether the resource recovers **naturally** over time.
>
>   (Natural Resources, Line 7)
>
> - Whether it is a renewable or non-renewable resource, we must protect and use the given supplies **wisely**.
>
>   (Natural Resources, Line 17)
>
> - The average temperatures on Earth have risen **significantly** over the last century.
>
>   (Global Warming, Line 1)

Choose the best position for the adverb provided in the parentheses and rewrite the sentence including the adverb.

1 Babies learn ① to speak ② by being exposed ③ to the language adults use. (naturally)

2 The ① government should react ② to ③ public opinion. (wisely)

3 The number of people ① in rural areas has decreased ② over three ③ consecutive years. (significantly)

B. The Usage of Adverbs ❷

> **Examples from the passage**
>
> • With the world **rapidly** changing, and large countries such as India and China developing, natural resources are being used at an extraordinary rate.
>
> (Natural Resources, Line 4)

Go through the passages in Unit 4 and find the two sentences below. Complete the sentences with the appropriate adverbs.

1 Dams are often essential for the daily survival of _____ populated areas.

2 Experts believe that global warming is also responsible for the _____ high frequency and intensity of hurricanes, heat waves and other extreme weather conditions.

Complete the following phrases with appropriate adverbs. There can be more than two answers for each phrase.

• carefully   • highly   • noticeably   • truly   • slowly

3 a _____ innovative idea

4 a _____ dangerous accident

5 a _____ arranged plan

UNIT 05
Political Science

•• Search! Search!

Find out about the topics using the Internet.
<u>Smoking Bans</u>, **The United Nations, The Beginning of Democracy, Monarchies**

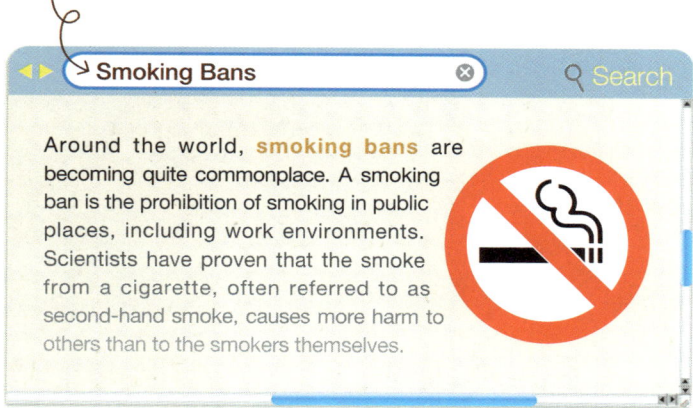

•• Target iBT TOEFL Questions

Rhetorical Purpose Questions

- The author mentions _____ in order to...
- The author says/discusses _____ by (giving examples...)
- What's the function of paragraph X as it relates to the rest of the passage?

Practice 1

Warm Up

1 Smoking is harmful to one's health. Check (✔) the policies your government has adopted.

☐ To ban smoking on the street   ☐ To advertise no-smoking policies
☐ To ban smoking in workplaces   ☐ To ban advertising of cigarettes

Read the Passage

Your time (1st): _____ min, (2nd): _____ min

Smoking Bans

Around the world, smoking bans are becoming quite commonplace. A smoking ban is the prohibition of smoking in public places, including work environments. Scientists have proven that the smoke from a cigarette, often referred to as second-hand smoke, causes more harm to others than to the smokers themselves. This is because second-smoke goes unfiltered. Like smoking, second-smoke can lead to serious illnesses including, but not limited to, cancer and heart disease.

Though smoking bans seem to be only a recent trend, their history traces back to the Catholic Church in 1590 when Pope Urban VII declared that no one was allowed to smoke or carry tobacco in or around the church. During the Nazi Party's reign in Germany in the 1930s and 1940s, smoking was banned in every university, post office and hospital. Today, however, it is the United States that is considered a true example of a smoke-free world. Nearly half of its states have already banned smoking in public. In 2007, Great Britain made similar regulations, and even 'cigarette-happy' cities like Paris are following the trend.

Though smoking bans are considered to be against smokers, the benefits are tremendous. The most noticeable is the improvement in health amongst the general public. In turn, this means lower healthcare costs and an increase in productivity in the workplace. Moreover, accidental fires can be reduced and streets can be cleaner. Though it may take time for many societies to embrace smoking bans, they will become more widespread and lead to a happier, healthier and more productive world.

Target iBT TOEFL Questions

1. In paragraph 2, the author mentions the Nazi Party's reign in order to
   - Ⓐ insist that smoking bans are a recent trend
   - Ⓑ explain how smoking bans began
   - Ⓒ add an explanation on the history of smoking bans

2. The word embrace in the passage is closest in meaning to
   - Ⓐ include
   - Ⓑ create
   - Ⓒ find

iBT TOEFL Vocabulary

Fill in the blanks with the appropriate words.

#	Word	Definition
1		**adj** happening more often than normal, not unusual
2		**n** the act of stopping something from being done
3		**n** a rule, a principle
4		**adj** very large in size
5		**adj** happening unexpectedly

- tremendous
- accidental
- commonplace
- prohibition
- regulation

Wrap Up

A Complete the sentences with the appropriate words.

- prohibition
- accidental
- regulation
- commonplace
- tremendous

1 It is now _____ to use the Internet at home.

2 Employing children is banned by the _____ of human rights.

3 The organization received _____ support from all over the world.

4 The fire was _____ ; there was no evidence which shows it was planned.

5 The environmentalists insist a _____ on the use of pesticides.

B Check (✔) whether the sentences are True (T) or False (F) according to the passage <Smoking Bans>.

1 According to a smoking ban, people are not allowed to smoke in public places. T ___ F ___

2 Smoking bans are a recent trend. T ___ F ___

3 By not allowing smoking in the workplace, productivity can be raised. T ___ F ___

4 The first smoking ban began during the Nazi party's reign. T ___ F ___

5 There are a lot of benefits that smoking bans provide. T ___ F ___

Practice 2

Warm Up

1 These are some of the names of international organizations. Talk about the purpose of each organization.

- UNICEF (United Nations International Children's Emergency Fund)
- UN (The United Nations)
- WHO (World Health Organization)

Read the Passage

Your time (1st): _____ min, (2nd): _____ min

The United Nations

The United Nations, often referred to as the UN, is an organization that works to mediate and enforce international law, security, peace and the protection of human rights, among many other things. Initially, though, the United Nations was founded in 1945, just after World War II, as a peacekeeping body, replacing the former League of Nations. With its headquarters in New York City, it manages to work together with nearly 200 countries as members, known as Member States, allowing for international dialogue and setting global goals.

The UN's efforts, along with its various 'sister' organizations, mainly work to improve our daily lives in the most important of ways, whether it means protecting the environment, fighting deadly diseases such as AIDS or working to solve the epidemic that spreads across a large part of the world. In recent years, a great deal of the UN's energy has been dedicated to bringing down violence against humanity, along with lowering the global warming effect.

Participation was especially strong in the year 2000, when Member States gathered to plot out the document that sets worldwide goals for improving life throughout this planet. Some such goals are eliminating poverty and hunger, developing a primary school education system guaranteed to all, creating equality for women and reducing child death rates. The more countries collaborate, the faster we will be able to solve the problems that spread across the world we live in.

Target iBT TOEFL Questions

1 What is the function of paragraph 1 as it relates to the rest of the passage?

Ⓐ It gives general information about the United Nations.
Ⓑ It describes the detailed roles of the United Nations.
Ⓒ It shows why the United Nations became popular after its foundation.

2 In paragraph 2, the author discusses UN's efforts by

Ⓐ introducing UN's future roles
Ⓑ comparing the efforts with those of its 'sister' organizations
Ⓒ listing examples of the efforts

iBT TOEFL Vocabulary

Fill in the blanks with the appropriate words.

1 _____	**v**	to make sure that people obey a rule
2 _____	**v**	to devote, to give entirely to someone or something
3 _____	**v**	to get rid of something
4 _____	**v**	to make certain of
5 _____	**n**	the quality of having the same rights
6 _____	**v**	to work together to make something

- collaborate
- guarantee
- dedicate
- enforce
- equality
- eliminate

Wrap Up

A Complete the sentences with the appropriate words.

- enforce
- collaborating
- equality
- eliminated
- dedicated
- guaranteed

1 In general, the policemen's main duty is to _____ the law.

2 Many have fought for women's _____ in the workplace for past centuries.

3 The player has been _____ from the tournament for not following the rules.

4 The environmental group has been _____ with the teachers to provide environmental education to young children.

5 Free elementary education is _____ by law.

6 The researchers have been _____ to developing a new vaccine.

B Complete the summary of the passage <The United Nations>.

The United Nations began as a _____ body in _____, replacing the former League of Nations. The UN now has nearly _____ Member States and its headquarters are in New York City. The UN mainly works to _____ our lives in many ways. The UN sets new goals in 2000. They include eliminating poverty and _____, developing a _____ school education system for all, creating equality for women and reducing child _____ rates.

Political Science •• 81

Test 1

The Beginning of Democracy

Democracy is a Greek word that literally translates as 'the rule of the people.' From 510 BC, Athens became the home of democracy from which its modern versions sprung. The Athenian democracy allowed citizens to vote on every law, including those related to foreign policy, military action and money for public projects. Whichever proposal received the most votes won. This is known as direct democracy.

[■A] To ensure the complete functioning of government, it was necessary to have public officials. [■B] All citizens interested in serving could sign up, regardless of their socio-economic status, and were chosen at random. [■C] There were thousands of public positions and each person could not hold the same position more than once. [■D] This drastically limited the power any one person could attain. Furthermore, citizens were expected to attend various assemblies each month to discuss the relevant issues. It was considered every citizen's civic duty to attend, and those caught not attending were fined.

However, like anything, the Athenian democracy had its faults. There was no constitution to grant stability, so even though a right was granted one day, it could be cancelled the next day. Additionally, women and slaves did not have the full rights of a citizen and, thus, were not allowed to vote. Ultimately, it was the time-consuming nature of this form of government that led to the downfall of Athens' democracy. Men had work to do and lives to lead. They could not dedicate all of their time to governing. As a result, the representation-based form of democracy, which we see today, emerged.

* constitution: a set of basic laws that a country is governed by

1 The word its in the passage refers to

 Ⓐ democracy
 Ⓑ a Greek word
 Ⓒ Anthens
 Ⓓ home

2 In paragraph 1, the author explains direct democracy by

 Ⓐ comparing it with the Athenian democracy
 Ⓑ emphasizing the roles of citizens
 Ⓒ explaining some features of it
 Ⓓ defining the word 'democracy'

3 According to paragraph 1, which of the following is NOT true of direct democracy?

 Ⓐ It began in Athens.
 Ⓑ It is the first form of today's democracy.
 Ⓒ Citizens gather money for public projects.
 Ⓓ Every law is determined by voting.

4 Look at the four squares [■] that indicate where the following sentence could be added to the passage.

The selection of officials relied on a lottery system.

Where would the sentence best fit?

5 The word drastically in the passage is closest in meaning to

 Ⓐ extremely
 Ⓑ rapidly
 Ⓒ nearly
 Ⓓ mainly

Political Science •• 83

6 The word attain in the passage is closest in meaning to

   Ⓐ experience
   Ⓑ achieve
   Ⓒ create
   Ⓓ buy

7 Which of the following best expresses the essential information in the highlighted sentence in the passage? Incorrect answer choices change the meaning in important ways or leave out essential information.

   It was considered every citizen's civic duty to attend, and those caught not attending were fined.

   Ⓐ Every citizen had to pay money for not attending various assemblies because it was their duty.
   Ⓑ If the citizens who did not attend meetings were caught, they were fined for not following their duty.
   Ⓒ Some citizens had to pay money for the assemblies because it was their civic duty.
   Ⓓ The citizens who were assigned to attend the meetings had to pay money.

8 According to paragraph 3, which of the following is NOT mentioned as a fault of the Athenian democracy?

   Ⓐ Their political positions were not stable.
   Ⓑ Some groups of people were not allowed to vote.
   Ⓒ It had the time-consuming nature of governing.
   Ⓓ It changed from direct democracy to the representation-based democracy.

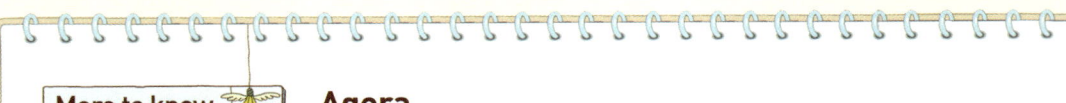

| More to know | **Agora** |

In early Greek history, the agora was mainly used as a public place of assembly. Free-born males and land-owners who were citizens gathered in the agora to hear statements of the ruling king and participate in the policy making processes. Later in Greek history, the agora served as a marketplace.

Test 2

Monarchies

A monarchy is a form of government in which one person rules an entire state. A monarchy is generally hereditary or rather, passed down within a single family. The world's most well-known monarchy is the United Kingdom. However, there are as many as forty other countries that currently embrace this governmental system as well. Monarchies came into existence from ancient tribal governments and dynasties. The traditional role and power held by a monarch have changed over the centuries, thus creating two major types: absolute monarchies and constitutional monarchies.

An absolute monarchy is the most traditional type. It can be traced back in history thousands of years, but is no longer very common. An absolute monarchy is when a state, both government and citizens, is led solely by the monarch. In such situations, a monarch pulls together a cabinet, which advises him or her as to what is best for the state, but has absolutely no power to make final decisions. Countries such as Saudi Arabia, Oman and Bhutan are still under the reign of absolute monarchs.

The most common type of monarchy is known as a constitutional monarchy. This is when a monarch's power is shared with a congress or parliament. The power of a monarch within a constitutional monarchy varies from state to state, with some having more than others. In some monarchies, the monarch plays an active role in ruling their nation. In others such as the United Kingdom, they simply serve as <u>figureheads</u>, though they have the power to <u>overrule</u> any decision made by parliament or congress.

* **figurehead:** nomial head, a leader of a group who has little power
* **overrule:** to cancel, to reverse a decision

1 According to paragraph 1, which of the following is NOT mentioned about a monarchy?

Ⓐ Up to 40 countries follow the governmental system today.
Ⓑ It is passed down within family members.
Ⓒ It is originated from tribal governments and dynasties.
Ⓓ It has many advantages.

2 The word solely in the passage is closest in meaning to

Ⓐ simply　　Ⓑ consequently　　Ⓒ clearly　　Ⓓ entirely

3 The word absolutely in the passage is closest in meaning to

Ⓐ perfectly　　Ⓑ apparently　　Ⓒ necessarily　　Ⓓ particularly

4 Which of the following best expresses the essential information in the highlighted sentence in the passage? Incorrect answer choices change the meaning in important ways or leave out essential information.

The traditional role and power held by a monarch have changed over the centuries, thus creating two major types.

Ⓐ The role and power of a monarch have changed into two major types.
Ⓑ A monarch became to have a different position in the major two types as it developed.
Ⓒ Over the course of hundreds of years, the role and power of monarchs have changed, and today monarchies are categorized into two major types.
Ⓓ A monarch holds the traditional role and power in two major types.

5 In the passage, the author explains monarchies by

Ⓐ explaining the role of a monarch
Ⓑ categorizing them into two types
Ⓒ providing their history
Ⓓ showing the differences among countries

6 What is the function of paragraph 1 as it relates to the rest of the passage?

Ⓐ It summarizes the features of an absolute monarchy.
Ⓑ It shows the reasons two types of monarchies have been created.
Ⓒ It gives a definition and general overview of a monarchy.
Ⓓ It highlights the power and roles of a monarch.

7 Directions: Complete the table below about the two types of monarchies. Match the statements to the appropriate category. TWO of the answer choices will NOT be used.

Answer Choices

Ⓐ The monarch rules a certain part of the country in this system.
Ⓑ Saudi Arabia, Oman and Bhutan have this type of monarchy.
Ⓒ It is the most traditional type.
Ⓓ It is the most common type of monarchy.
Ⓔ A cabinet can advise the monarch.
Ⓕ More and more countries follow this type of monarchy.
Ⓖ Sometimes, the monarch is simply a figurehead in this system.

Absolute monarchy
-
-
-

Constitutional monarchy
-
-

More to know   **Queen Elizabeth II**

Elizabeth II (born 1926) became a queen following the death of her father, George VI, in 1952. Ever since then she has been the United Kingdom's respected monarch, a head of state. In 2002, she celebrated her 50 years on the throne and in 2006 her 80th birthday.

Reading Helper

A. ...ing

> **Examples from the passage**
>
> - Like smoking, second-smoke can lead to serious illnesses **including**, but not limited to, cancer and heart disease.
>   (Smoking Bans, Line 7)
>
> - Initially, though, the United Nations was founded in 1945, just after World War II, as a peacekeeping body, **replacing** the former League of Nations.
>   (The United Nations, Line 3)
>
> - The Athenian democracy allowed citizens to vote on every law, **including** those related to foreign policy, military action and money for public projects.
>   (The Beginning of Democracy, Line 3)

Choose one sentence that is NOT true according to the sentence in bold.

1. Like smoking, second-smoke can lead to serious illnesses including, but not limited to, cancer and heart disease.

    Ⓐ Only second-smoke causes serious illnesses.
    Ⓑ The examples of serious illnesses from second-smoke cannot be limited to cancer and heart disease.
    Ⓒ The illnesses that second-hand smoke can lead include cancer and heart disease.

2. Initially, though, the United Nations was founded in 1945, just after World War II, as a peacekeeping body, replacing the former League of Nations.

    Ⓐ The United Nations was founded right after Word War II.
    Ⓑ The United Nations originally began as a peacekeeping organization.
    Ⓒ The former version of League of Nations was the United Nations.

3 The Athenian democracy allowed citizens to vote on every law, including those related to foreign policy, military action and money for public projects.

Ⓐ In the Athenian democracy, citizens could vote on every law related to foreign policy, military action and money for public projects.

Ⓑ In the Athenian democracy, every law was related to foreign policy, military action and money for public projects.

Ⓒ The laws that citizens could vote in the Athenian democracy included the laws related to foreign policy, military action and money for public projects.

UNIT 06
Arts

•• Search! Search!

Find out about the topics using the Internet.
The Violin, Vincent Van Gogh, The Globe Theatre, Puppetry

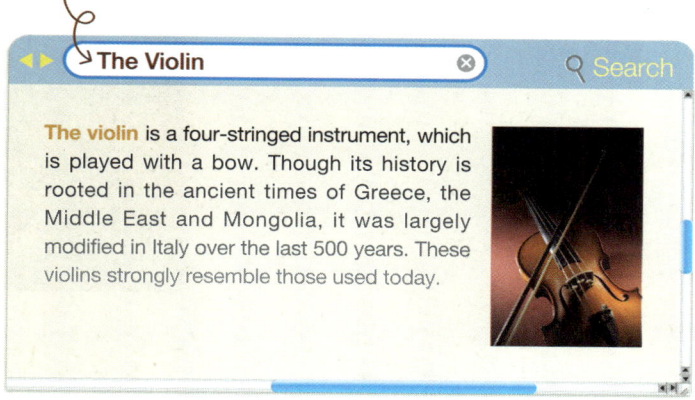

•• Target iBT TOEFL Questions

Insert Text Questions

Look at the four squares [■] that indicate where the following sentence could be added to the passage.

A sentence
Where would the sentence best fit?

Practice 1

Warm Up

1 Complete the features of the violin with the appropriate words.

- Italy
- four
- bow
- stringed
- smallest

- Has _____ strings and a hollow body
- Played with a _____
- Developed in _____
- The _____ and highest-pitched member of the _____ instrument family

Read the Passage

Your time (1st): ____ min, (2nd): ____ min

The Violin

The violin is a four-stringed instrument, which is played with a bow. Though its history is rooted in the ancient times of Greece, the Middle East and Mongolia, it was largely modified in Italy over the last 500 years. These violins strongly resemble those used today.

[■A] The violin belongs to the string family. [■B] It is known for its high-pitch and soundboard, which is the wooden box where the moving air from string vibrations resonates to create sound. [■C] The intensity of the sound emitted by a violin is determined by the way the player presses the strings on the fingerboard. [■D]

[■E] Cremona was the home of the most famous violinmakers. [■F] Between 16th and 18th centuries, the Guaneri, Stradivari and Amati violin shops were all located in the city. [■G] The different parts of their violins were made from various woods including maple and ebony. [■H] The strings were originally dried and stretched sheep guts, but modern strings are often created with synthetic materials or stranded steel.

The violin offers a wide range of sound, which is why it suits solo performances as well as symphony orchestras. In Italy, its popularity grew slowly, but it was Louis XIII of France who was largely responsible for the violin's rise in popularity, when he incorporated 24 of them into his grand orchestra in 1826. To this day, the violin remains one of the most popular instruments around the world.

Target iBT TOEFL Questions

1. Look at the four squares [■A]~[■D] that indicate where the following sentence could be added to the passage.

   Other instruments in this family include the viola, cello and upright bass.

   Where would the sentence best fit?

2. Look at the four squares [■E]~[■H] that indicate where the following sentence could be added to the passage.

   They still are the most highly sought after.

   Where would the sentence best fit?

iBT TOEFL Vocabulary

Fill in the blanks with the appropriate words.

1 _____	**adv** mainly
2 _____	**v** to change something slightly from its original form
3 _____	**v** to give off light, gas, or heat
4 _____	**adv** in the first place, at first
5 _____	**v** to include something as a part

- originally
- largely
- modify
- incorporate
- emit

Wrap Up

A Complete the sentences with the appropriate words.

- largely
- incorporates
- emits
- originally
- modified

1. Our success was _____ due to all the efforts made by the members.

2. The building _____ had nine floors and a tenth was added later.

3. The plan has been _____ according to new needs of the consumers.

4. Like the sun, the moon also _____ light.

5. The digital camera _____ new features for clear images.

B Check (✔) whether the sentences are True (T) or False (F) according to the passage <The Violin>.

1. The history of the violin began in Italy. — T ☐ F ☐

2. The intensity of the sound of the violin depends on how hard the player presses the strings. — T ☐ F ☐

3. Cremona is the city that was famous for its woods. — T ☐ F ☐

4. Modern strings use sheep guts to create sound. — T ☐ F ☐

5. The violin gained popularity when Louis XIII used 24 violins in his orchestra. — T ☐ F ☐

Practice 2

Warm Up

1 Are you familiar with the following names? Who are they?

- Vincent Van Gogh
- Paul Gauguin
- Claude Oscar Monet

2 Search for some of Van Gogh's famous paintings.

Read the Passage

Your time (1st): _____ min, (2nd): _____ min

Vincent Van Gogh

<The Church at Auvers>

Vincent Van Gogh, now one of the world's most famed painters, received very little recognition for his talents and work during his life. He was born in Holland in 1853, but spent a large part of his life in Belgium and France. Before pursuing art full-time in 1881, he attempted a variety of jobs, including ones such as a bookstore clerk, French tutor and a preacher.

[■A] Then in 1886, he moved to Paris and worked with his brother, who managed an art gallery. [■B] Eventually, he studied painting under Fernand Cormon, and thus met esteemed painters such as Gauguin and Monet. [■C] Despite his connections in the art world, Van Gogh sold only one painting while alive and lived much of his life in poverty. [■D] He even suffered from aggression and general insanity. In one of his violent fits, he attacked his dear friend, Gauguin, but he ended up chopping off his own ear.

Shortly thereafter, Van Gogh ended up in a mental hospital in Saint-Remy. [■E] In the end, he was released under the requirement that he receive care from a specific doctor. [■F] However, only two months after he got out of the hospital in 1890, Van Gogh killed himself.

[■G] Though he had a short and often tragic life, it was highly productive. [■H] He may not have gained recognition during his life, but today his paintings are some of the most expensive and desired pieces of art all around the world.

Target iBT TOEFL Questions

1 Look at the four squares [■A]~[■D] that indicate where the following sentence could be added to the passage.

Furthermore, he had poor health.

Where would the sentence best fit?

2 Look at the four squares [■E]~[■H] that indicate where the following sentence could be added to the passage.

He produced over 800 paintings and countless drawings.

Where would the sentence best fit?

iBT TOEFL Vocabulary

Fill in the blanks with the appropriate words.

1. _____ **adj** aggressive, acting with great force
2. _____ **adj** respected, admired
3. _____ **n** violent action
4. _____ **n** the state of being acknowledged
5. _____ **adj** very bad, terrible, miserable

- tragic
- violent
- aggression
- recognition
- esteemed

Wrap Up

A Complete the sentences with the appropriate words.

- violent
- tragic
- aggression
- recognition
- esteemed

1 It is widely known that violence on TV may cause _____ behavior in children.

2 Pierre-Auguste Renoir is one of the most _____ artists of the nineteenth century.

3 The professor's death is a _____ loss for the field of Astronomy.

4 Alcohol abuse can be a possible cause of _____ .

5 The soldiers received _____ for their contribution in the war.

B Check (✔) whether the sentences are True (T) or False (F) according to the passage <Vincent Van Gogh>.

1 Van Gogh was popular when he was alive.   T ☐   F ☐

2 Van Gogh moved to Paris in his thirties.   T ☐   F ☐

3 Van Gogh managed an art gallery with his brother.   T ☐   F ☐

4 Van Gogh was once hospitalized due to his insanity.   T ☐   F ☐

5 Van Gogh taught painting to Fernand Cormon.   T ☐   F ☐

The Globe Theatre

During the reign of Queen Elizabeth I, the theater scene in London was booming. One man was largely responsible for this: William Shakespeare. He was the most respected playwright in England. His theater company was at the forefront of the golden age of Elizabethan theater. They built the Globe Theatre in 1599, and it barely lasted 15 years before being destroyed by a fire. However, it was reconstructed at the same site.

The Globe could hold up to 3,000 audience members and was built in a similar fashion to Greek amphitheaters. [■A] It was an open-air stage, which meant it relied on good weather conditions for the plays to be performed. [■B] Though the Globe was extremely large, it had a very basic set. [■C] The stage was plain, there was no lighting and very few props were used. [■D]

[■E] Shakespeare's success was largely because his plays were understandable by everyone, regardless of their level of education. [■F] Moreover, tickets were affordable. [■G] There were also three different levels of stadium style seating for those who could afford to pay more. [■H]

Eventually, the Puritans, who were closing all venues of entertainment, including all theaters, brought the Globe's glory to an end in 1642. In Shakespeare's honor, Queen Elizabeth II ordered a replica to be constructed near the original site. People's love of Shakespeare continues to grow and he is regarded as the greatest playwright to ever exist.

* **forefront:** the leading position
* **prop:** support, column

1 The word site in the passage is closest in meaning to

Ⓐ level
Ⓑ street
Ⓒ system
Ⓓ location

2 According to paragraphs 1 and 2, which of the following is true of the Globe?

　Ⓐ Queen Elizabeth I encouraged Shakespeare to build the theater.
　Ⓑ Its stage was small and simple.
　Ⓒ 3,000 members participated to build the theater.
　Ⓓ It was destroyed by a fire in 1614 but was rebuilt.

3 The word extremely in the passage is closest in meaning to

　Ⓐ practically
　Ⓑ finely
　Ⓒ highly
　Ⓓ seriously

4 Look at the four squares [■A]~[■D] that indicate where the following sentence could be added to the passage.

Shakespeare's plays were so well-written that props were unnecessary in telling the stories.

Where would the sentence best fit?

5 According to paragraph 3, Shakespeare's success was because

　Ⓐ his plays were easy to understand
　Ⓑ his plays were mainly about education
　Ⓒ his theater had three different levels
　Ⓓ the tickets for his plays were free

6 According to paragraph 3, it can be inferred that

　Ⓐ The prices for the tickets were different according to the seats.
　Ⓑ Actors used easy languages for the common people.
　Ⓒ The common people were not allowed to see the plays.
　Ⓓ People needed to stand up to see Shakespeare's plays.

7 Look at the four squares [■E]~[■H] that indicate where the following sentence could be added to the passage.

Even people of the lower classes could pay a penny to stand in the area located in front of the stage.

Where would the sentence best fit?

8 Which of the following best expresses the essential information in the highlighted sentence in the passage? Incorrect answer choices change the meaning in important ways or leave out essential information.

==Eventually the Puritans, who were closing all venues of entertainment, including all theaters, brought the Globe's glory to an end in 1642.==

Ⓐ The Puritans destroyed the Globe in 1642 including all theaters.
Ⓑ In 1642, the Puritans banned all types of entertainment including the Globe.
Ⓒ The Globe had to be closed in 1642 as the Puritans forced all theaters to close.
Ⓓ All theaters except the Globe were closed as the Puritans banned all types of entertainment.

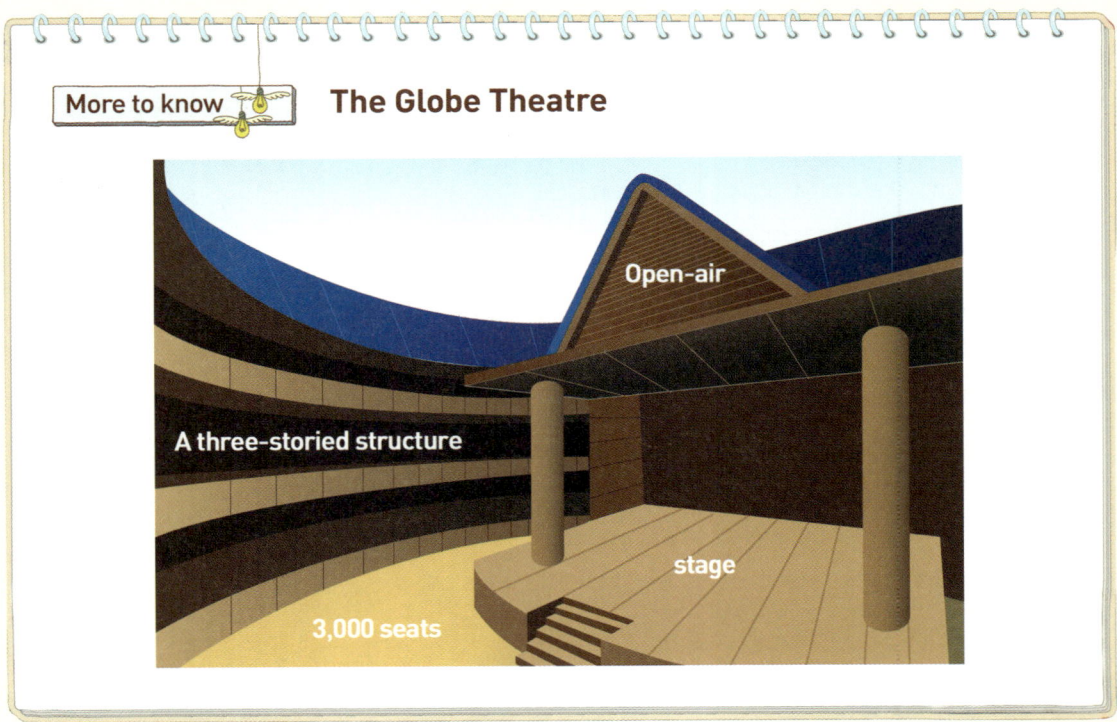

More to know

The Globe Theatre

Open-air
A three-storied structure
stage
3,000 seats

Test 2

Puppetry

Puppetry, popular for many centuries with various cultures, is the oldest performance art in the world. It involves telling stories through animating objects or dolls that would not otherwise move on their own. In fourth century BC the Greek philosopher, Plato, first mentioned puppetry in his writings, but it is believed that puppetry was created over 30,000 years ago. It has since been used for entertainment, as well as for ceremonies and rituals.

The earliest puppetry was in the form of shadow puppets. This is when shadows are cast upon a lit wall in order to tell a story. Shadow puppets were used around the world, especially favored in Asia and the Middle East, and eventually evolved into a performance using actual dolls. Dolls made of clay and ivory were used and puppet stands were commonly seen along the sides of streets, especially in places such as France, Italy, Germany and Russia. On the whole, puppetry's popularity increased on the European continent. European styles even changed the way Native Americans used puppets.

[■A] Initially in Europe, puppetry was often performed as a satire and used to make political statements. [■B] Meanwhile, churches began to follow the eastern tradition of using puppetry to teach morals. [■C] By the eighteenth century, Europeans considered puppetry to be a serious art, and operas and tragic plays were performed with puppets. [■D] Puppetry, though not as commonly seen as in the past, is still a thriving art.

* **satire:** mockery, irony, ridiculous

1 In paragraph 1, why does the author mention Plato ?

　Ⓐ To provide historical evidence about puppetry's origin
　Ⓑ To explain why puppetry was popular
　Ⓒ To emphasize who first developed puppetry
　Ⓓ To reveal that puppetry was used for entertainment

2 The word favored in the passage is closest in meaning to

　Ⓐ popular
　Ⓑ unique
　Ⓒ realistic
　Ⓓ similar

3 The word commonly in the passage is closest in meaning to

　Ⓐ gradually
　Ⓑ usually
　Ⓒ easily
　Ⓓ constantly

4 According to paragraph 2, which of the following is NOT true of shadow puppetry?

　Ⓐ They were the earlier form of puppetry.
　Ⓑ They were especially welcomed in Asia and the Middle East.
　Ⓒ European shadow puppetry affected the way Asians used puppets.
　Ⓓ They were used in many countries.

5 Look at the four squares [■] that indicate where the following sentence could be added to the passage.

Presently, puppetry is often combined with television such as Sesame Street.

Where would the sentence best fit?

6 Which of the following best expresses the essential information in the highlighted sentence in the passage? Incorrect answer choices change the meaning in important ways or leave out essential information.

Puppetry, though not as commonly seen as in the past, is still a thriving art.

Ⓐ Puppetry has been successfully survived as a common art form.
Ⓑ Although puppetry is not as famous as before, it is still thriving as an art.
Ⓒ Puppetry is an energetic art form though it is not popular as before.
Ⓓ Although puppetry was once a popular art form, it has now disappeared.

7 In the passage, the author explains puppetry by

Ⓐ comparing puppetry with tragic plays
Ⓑ listing the countries still using puppetry
Ⓒ introducing the philosopher who created puppetry
Ⓓ discussing the historical changes of puppetry over time

More to know | **Puppetry in India**

Besides providing entertainment, puppetry is also used for conveying meaningful messages. India has a rich heritage of puppetry. The history of puppetry in India began around the 5th century BC. The puppet shows in India mostly dealt with the histories of kings, princes and heroes. They also dealt with religious themes and mythological stories.

Reading Helper

A. Though

> **Examples from the passage**
>
> - **Though** he had a short and often tragic life, it was highly productive.
>
>   (Vincent Van Gogh, Line 18)
>
> - **Though** the Globe was extremely large, it had a very basic set.   (The Globe Theatre, Line 10)
>
> - Puppetry, **though** not as commonly seen as in the past, is still a thriving art.
>
>   (Puppetry, Line 21)

Rewrite the sentences using *though* as seen in the example.

> The Globe was extremely large, but it had a very basic set.
> ⇨ **Though the Globe was extremely large, it had a very basic set.**

1 The experiment was not successful, but the researchers found important clues on the problem.

2 Mozart died at the age of 35, but he composed more than 600 works.

B. During

Examples from the passage

- Vincent Van Gogh, now one of the world's most famed painters, received very little recognition for his talents and work **during** his life. (Vincent Van Gogh, Line 1)

- **During** the reign of Queen Elizabeth I, the theater scene in London was booming. (The Globe Theatre, Line 1)

Complete the following sentences by combining the expressions provided in the parenthesis and the word *during*.

1 The book is about the two soldiers' friendship. (World War II)

2 Butterflies change their appearance several times. (lifetime)

3 Students can participate in many interesting programs that are provided by the community center. (summer vacation)

UNIT 07
Earth Science

•• Search! Search!

Find out about the topics using the Internet.
The Earth's Structure, Weathering & Erosion, Sea Breezes & Land Breezes, Clouds Types

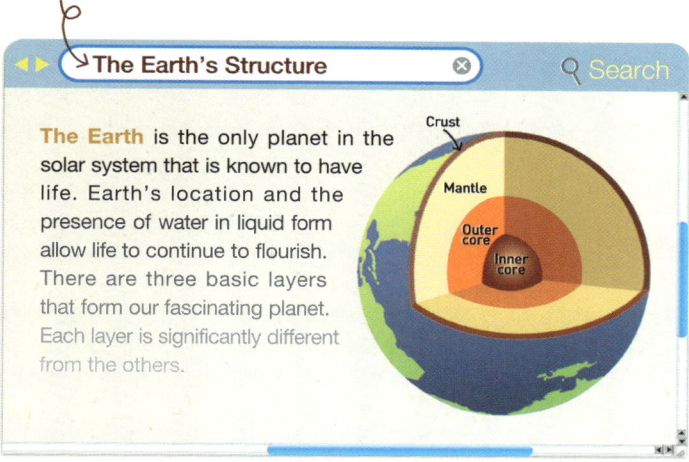

•• Target iBT TOEFL Questions

Categorization Questions

Directions: Complete the table below about the two types of _____ discussed in the passage. Match the appropriate phrases/statements to the types of _____ with which they are associated. Two of the answer choices will NOT be used.

Answer Choices

Ⓐ ~ Ⓖ

Category 1
- _____
- _____
- _____

Category 2
- _____
- _____

Practice 1

Warm Up

1 What are destructive forces of nature? List at least two.

☐ hurricane   ☐ tornado   ☐ _____   ☐ _____

Have you experienced any of those? Check (✔) the ones you have experienced and talk about their effects on the earth.

Read the Passage

Your time (1st): _____ min, (2nd): _____ min

Weathering & Erosion

The Earth's surface changes every day. Natural occurrences are responsible for these changes and the reshaping of its surface. Extreme conditions such as volcanic eruptions and earthquakes can create a great deal of changes. However, weathering and erosion are slower and much more gradual processes.

Weathering is the process in which large rocks are broken down into smaller rocks because of water, wind and glaciers. However, the location of these rocks is the same and they simply remain close to one another. If small rocks continue to break down, they eventually become dirt. Such weathering often stems from the freezing and <u>thawing</u> of water on the Earth's surface. Additionally, weathering can occur through chemical reactions. Water dissolves minerals in certain types of rocks, a process which leads to the formation of different land features, such as caves, fjords and streams.

Erosion is when there is a permanent removal of rocks and soil by wind, water or humans' use of land. Moving water is the leading cause of erosion. Rivers carry over 20 billion small rocks to the ocean each year. Erosion by wind results in the creation of landforms by blowing sand, soil and other <u>sediments</u> away. Unfortunately, the erosion humans are creating, such as deforestation and constant construction, is extremely harmful to the ecosystem. These practices remove soil, nutrients and organisms that are necessary for the survival of smaller ecosystems on Earth.

* **thaw:** to become liquid, to dissolve
* **sediment:** matter that has been produced by natural processes

Target iBT TOEFL Questions

1 Directions: Complete the table below about the natural occurrences. Match the appropriate phrases to the types with which they are associated. TWO of the answer choices will NOT be used.

Answer Choices

Ⓐ occurs extremely quickly
Ⓑ is caused by water, wind and glaciers
Ⓒ can occur by deforestation
Ⓓ often comes from the freezing and melting of water
Ⓔ is harmful to the ecosystem
Ⓕ can form caves, fjords and streams
Ⓖ is mainly caused by moving water

Weathering

- _____
- _____
- _____

Erosion

- _____
- _____

iBT TOEFL Vocabulary

Fill in the blanks with the appropriate words.

1 _____ **n** an event that happens
2 _____ **v** to change the form again
3 _____ **adj** ultimate, very great
4 _____ **adj** happening slowly
5 _____ **v** to melt, to thaw
6 _____ **adj** ever-lasting, lasting without change

- gradual
- dissolve
- occurrence
- reshape
- extreme
- permanent

Wrap Up

A Complete the sentences with the appropriate words.

- occurrence
- reshaped
- extreme
- permanent
- dissolve
- gradual

1 There has been a _____ increase over time in sea level.

2 Oil does not _____ in water.

3 For the last century, a great number of people have suffered from _____ poverty.

4 The doves have been a _____ symbol of peace in some countries.

5 Virus infection of a computer system is a common _____ these days.

6 The land has been _____ by weather.

B Complete the summary note of the passage <Weathering & Erosion>.

Paragraph 1: The Earth's surface changes every day as a result of natural occurrences.
(1) extreme changes: volcanic eruptions, _____
(2) slow changes: weathering, _____

Paragraph 2: Weathering
- Definition: the process in which large rocks are broken down into smaller pieces due to water, _____ and glaciers
- can occur through _____ reactions
  ⇨ creates caves, fjords and streams

Paragraph 3: Erosion
- Definition: the condition in which the rocks and soil are removed by wind, _____ or human's use of land
- Unlike natural occurrences, the erosion created by humans can _____ the ecosystem.

Practice 2

Warm Up

1 Read the words below and check (✔) for which layer they are used to describe.

• thick   • flexible   • softer   • constant movement   • shifting

☐ crust   ☐ mantle   ☐ core

Read the Passage

Your time (1st): _____ min, (2nd): _____ min

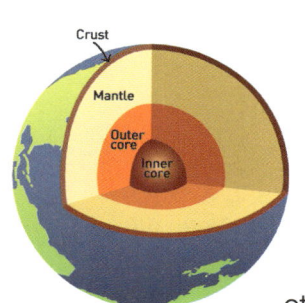

The Earth's Structure

The Earth is the only planet in the solar system that is known to have life. Earth's location and the presence of water in liquid form allow life to continue to flourish. There are three basic layers that form our fascinating planet. Each layer is significantly different from the others.

The outermost layer is known as the crust. The crust includes the Earth's surface such as the continents and oceans. The crust is formed through volcanic activity. Its thickness is inconsistent and can run as deep as 75 kilometers.

The layer below the crust is known as the mantle. Almost 70% of the Earth's matter is found in the mantle, as it is nearly 3,000 kilometers thick. Unlike the crust, which is hard, the mantle is a bit more flexible. The further into the mantle, the softer the rock gets. Under the softest layer there is constant movement and shifting of large sheets of rock.

The innermost layer is called the core and is divided into two parts: the inner core and the outer core. The outer core is mainly made of hot liquid iron and nickel. Combined with the Earth's rotation, this layer creates our planet's magnetic field. Meanwhile, the inner core is made of solid iron and nickel. This is the only part of Earth in which extreme temperatures exist. These extreme temperatures exist in order to keep the metals of the outer core in liquid form. Ultimately, the entire core of the Earth is approximately 3,500 kilometers deep.

Target iBT TOEFL Questions

1 Directions: Complete the table below about the Earth's structure. Match the appropriate phrases to the types of layers with which they are associated. TWO of the answer choices will NOT be used.

Answer Choices

Ⓐ is divided into two parts
Ⓑ is the outermost layer of the Earth
Ⓒ is located under the crust
Ⓓ is formed by volcanic eruptions
Ⓔ is the layer below mantle
Ⓕ is softer as it is close to the core
Ⓖ is around 3,500 kilometers deep

Core
-
-
-

Mantle
-
-

iBT TOEFL Vocabulary

Fill in the blanks with the appropriate words.

#		
1	**n**	the existence of someone or something
2	**v**	to thrive, to grow well
3	**adj**	changeable, unstable
4	**adv**	very, greatly, considerably
5	**adj**	capable of bending or being bent
6	**adj**	whole, all, total

- entire
- flexible
- significantly
- flourish
- presence
- inconsistent

Wrap Up

A Complete the sentences with the appropriate words.

- flourish
- presence
- inconsistent
- entire
- significantly
- flexible

1 The pole does not break easily since it is _____ .

2 The experts provided _____ different predictions on volcanic activity in the area.

3 Some people argue about the _____ of aliens on Mars.

4 Nearly the _____ population became to have access to health care and education.

5 The environmental campaign allowed plant life in the area to _____ once again.

6 The results of the two experiments were _____ , so scientists will be doing additional experiments.

B Complete the summary note of the passage <The Earth's Structure> by using the appropriate phrases.

❶ is formed through volcanic activity
❷ is nearly 3,000 kilometers thick
❸ keep the metals in liquid form
❹ creates our planet's magnetic field

Crust: (1) includes the Earth's surface
(2)
(3) its thickness is inconsistent

Mantle: (1)
(2) is not hard
(3) has constant movement and shifting of large sheets of rock

Core: A. Outer core: (1) is made of hot liquid iron and nickel
(2)

B. Inner core: (1) is made of solid iron and nickel
(2) has extreme temperatures to

Sea Breezes & Land Breezes

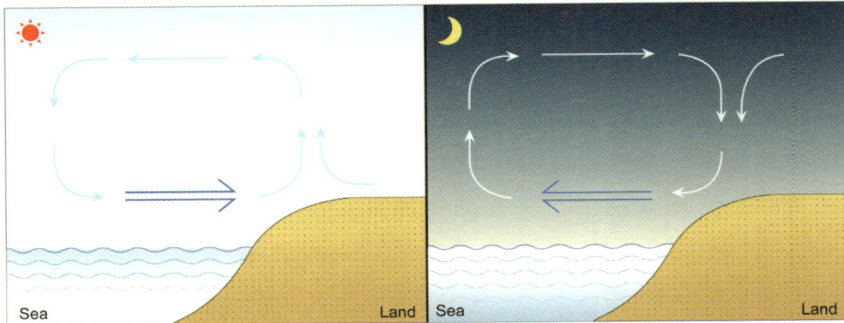

[■A] A light wind is often referred to as a breeze. [■B] Sea and land breezes are common weather occurrences in coastal areas. [■C] These two types of breezes are essentially opposites. They are determined by air circulation patterns during the day and night. [■D]

A land breeze is a wind that blows from land out towards a body of water. Water has a much greater heat capacity than soil. Thus, more heat is required to warm water than land, so land warms up and cools faster than water. As the sun sets at night, land cools faster than the sea. As the land cools, the air above it does too. As this happens, the air becomes dense and causes pressure to increase and thus, winds blow out to sea. The warm air above the sea rises and makes room for the cool air, which has blown out from the land.

During the day, the sun heats the land far quicker than it does the sea, so the land becomes warmer than the sea. Eventually, the warm air above the land rises and the cooler air above the sea moves inland. This wind that moves from the sea towards land is called a sea breeze. Sea breezes blow stronger than land breezes because they are less likely to be affected by the shape of coastal regions. This means that coastal regions experience sea breezes during the day and land breezes at night. It is important to understand, though, that both are considered to be localized weather patterns. They can always be overtaken by larger weather systems, especially intense storms.

1 Look at the four squares [■] that indicate where the following sentence could be added to the passage.

More specifically, these breezes occur due to a difference in the temperature of land and sea surfaces.

Where would the sentence best fit?

2 The word essentially in the passage is closest in meaning to

Ⓐ specifically
Ⓑ basically
Ⓒ mostly
Ⓓ finally

3 According to paragraph 2, what can be inferred about the relation between air and pressure?

Ⓐ Air moves from high pressure to low pressure.
Ⓑ Air is less likely to be affected by pressure.
Ⓒ High pressure causes air to become dense.
Ⓓ Low pressure creates high temperature in the air.

4 The word required in the passage is closet in meaning to

Ⓐ acquired
Ⓑ created
Ⓒ limited
Ⓓ needed

5 The word it in the passage refers to

Ⓐ the sun
Ⓑ land
Ⓒ sea
Ⓓ air

Earth Science •• 115

6 Which of the following best expresses the essential information in the highlighted sentence in the passage? Incorrect answer choices change the meaning in important ways or leave out essential information.

> They can always be overtaken by larger weather systems, especially intense storms.

Ⓐ Stronger weather changes such as storms can overtake larger weather systems.
Ⓑ Breezes can be overwhelmed by bigger weather changes such as storms.
Ⓒ Strong storms sometimes change the breeze systems.
Ⓓ Intense storms are especially larger weather systems than breezes.

7 Directions: Complete the table below about the two types of breezes. Match the appropriate phrases to the types with which they are associated. TWO of the answer choices will NOT be used.

Answer Choices

Ⓐ keeps temperatures high
Ⓑ is a wind from the sea to land
Ⓒ blows as the land cools rapidly at night
Ⓓ cools the sea
Ⓔ is caused because the land becomes warmer than the sea during the day
Ⓕ moves from land out towards the sea
Ⓖ results in cool days in coastal areas

Sea Breeze
-
-
-

Land Breeze
-
-

Test 2

Clouds Types

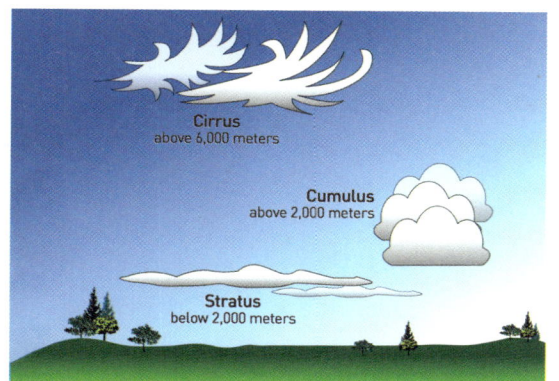

[■A] A cloud is water vapor that has collected in the sky and attached to small particles and dust floating in the air. [■B] This happens when warm air rises and cools. [■C] There are three major types of clouds: stratus, cumulus and cirrus. [■D]

Stratus clouds tend to spread out. They are made of many different layers and sometimes look as though they are blankets covering the sky. Their formation only occurs when a layer of warm air moves over a layer of cool air, and the warm air cools below its dew point. Stratus clouds are considered to be low-level clouds, which form at 2,000 meters or lower.

Cumulus clouds, on the other hand, look puffy like over-sized cotton balls floating in the sky. These clouds form when warm air rises. Cumulus clouds form higher in the sky than stratus clouds. They are generally found over 2,000 meters above the ground and can sometimes reach hundreds of meters in height. If cooled before its dew-point temperature, cumulus clouds may release rain, snow or ice.

Cirrus clouds, meaning *a curl of hair*, got their name from their appearance. They are typically thin and feather-like and are found at very high levels. Cirrus clouds form more than 6,000 meters above the ground. They can sometimes vary in color by assuming the color given off by the sun.

* particle: a small piece of anything

1. Look at the four squares [■] that indicate where the following sentence could be added to the passage.

   This can also happen when warm air passes over a colder area.

   Where would the sentence best fit?

2. The word Their in the passage refers to
   - Ⓐ stratus clouds
   - Ⓑ layers
   - Ⓒ blankets
   - Ⓓ cumulus clouds

3. In paragraph 3, why does the author mention cotton balls?
   - Ⓐ To describe the shape of cumulus clouds using examples
   - Ⓑ To compare the size of cumulus clouds with them
   - Ⓒ To explain how cumulus clouds are formed
   - Ⓓ To define the meaning of the word *puffy*

4. The word generally in the passage is closest in meaning to
   - Ⓐ always
   - Ⓑ surprisingly
   - Ⓒ normally
   - Ⓓ greatly

5. According to paragraph 3, which of the following is NOT mentioned about cumulus clouds?
   - Ⓐ They are formed when warm air moves slowly.
   - Ⓑ They have puffy shapes like cotton balls.
   - Ⓒ They form above 2,000 meters from the ground.
   - Ⓓ They may release rain, snow or ice.

6 Which of the following best expresses the essential information in the highlighted sentence in the passage? Incorrect answer choices change the meaning in important ways or leave out essential information.

<mark>They can sometimes vary in color by assuming the color given off by the sun.</mark>

Ⓐ They can occasionally have different colors since the sun accepts the color.
Ⓑ By taking the color from the sun, their color can differ at times.
Ⓒ Their colors can vary at times because they give off the color to the sun.
Ⓓ Their colors are different from each other by taking the color of the sun.

7 Directions: Complete the table below about the two types of clouds. Match the appropriate phrases to the types with which they are associated. TWO of the answer choices will NOT be used.

Answer Choices

Ⓐ have many different layers
Ⓑ are composed of snow
Ⓒ are formed at very high levels
Ⓓ are thin and look like feathers
Ⓔ look like blankets
Ⓕ form below 2,000 meters
Ⓖ are dark in color

Cirrus Clouds

-
-

Stratus Clouds

-
-
-

Earth Science •• 119

Reading Helper

A. Adverbs

> **Examples from the passage**
>
> • **Ultimately**, the entire core of the Earth is approximately 3,500 kilometers deep.
>
> (The Earth's Structure, Line 20)

Go through the passages in Unit 7 and find two more sentences that begin with an adverb such as *unfortunately*.

1. _____
   _____

   (The title of the passage: _____, Line ____)

2. _____
   _____

   (The title of the passage: _____, Line ____)

Rewrite the sentences you found above using the appropriate expressions from the box below.

| • at last • actually • furthermore • unluckily |

3. _____
   _____

4. _____
   _____

B. Passives

Examples from the passage

- They **are determined by** air circulation patterns during the day and night.
  (Sea Breezes & Land Breezes, Line 3)

- Sea breezes blow stronger than land breezes because they are less likely to **be affected by** the shape of coastal regions.
  (Sea Breezes & Land Breezes, Line 15)

- They can always **be overtaken by** larger weather systems, especially intense storms.
  (Sea Breezes & Land Breezes, Line 19)

Complete the sentences using the passive verb forms as seen in the example.

They can always overtake larger weather systems, especially intense storms.
⇨ They can always be overtaken by larger weather systems, especially intense storms.

1 The items can also categorize their shapes and sizes.

2 The questions answer (past tense) the experts.

3 The half of the electricity generated this year consume (past tense) industry.

UNIT 08
Human Body & Nutrition

•• Search! Search!

Find out about the topics using the Internet.
Vitamins, Salt and Health, The Importance of Fiber, Body Clocks

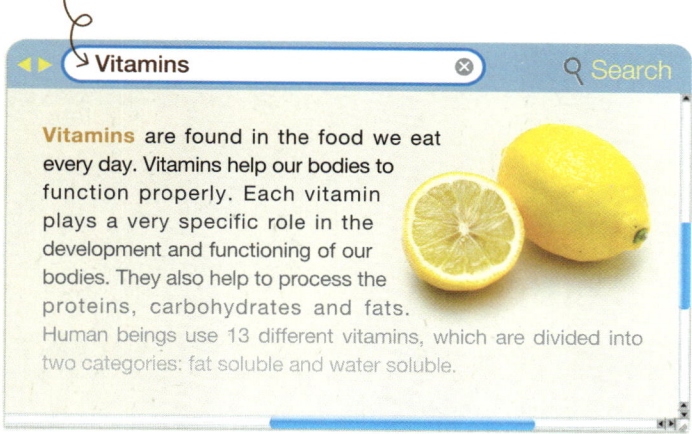

Vitamins are found in the food we eat every day. Vitamins help our bodies to function properly. Each vitamin plays a very specific role in the development and functioning of our bodies. They also help to process the proteins, carbohydrates and fats.
Human beings use 13 different vitamins, which are divided into two categories: fat soluble and water soluble.

•• Target iBT TOEFL Questions

Summary Questions

Directions: An introductory sentence for a brief summary of the passage is provided below. Complete the summary by selecting THREE answer choices that express important ideas in the passage. Some sentences do not belong in the summary because they express ideas that are not presented in the passage or are minor ideas in the passage.

An introductory sentence

-
-
-

Answer Choices

Ⓐ ~ Ⓕ

Practice 1

Warm Up

1 Do you like the following salty food? Why or why not?

- ham
- bacon
- popcorn
- potato chips

Read the Passage

Your time (1st): ___ min, (2nd): ___ min

Salt and Health

Salt consumption directly affects one's blood pressure and overall physical health. In fact, the more salt you consume, the higher your blood pressure will get. This is not only true for those with high blood pressure but also for those who are perfectly healthy. Not to mention, high salt intake can result in other physical problems, such as weight gain, bone density loss, and kidney disease. For this reason, it is strongly advised that everyone avoid eating excessive amounts of salt.

The recommended salt intake levels for an adult are below 5-6 grams (1 teaspoon) per day. This amount is considerably less than the national average for daily salt intake, which currently stands at double the recommended amount. This excessive intake is a primary cause of the high-blood pressure syndrome currently found across the United States.

Obviously, the problems caused by high salt intake can be solved by reducing the amount taken each day, and there are plenty of ways this can be accomplished. First, never add salt directly to your food, whether you are cooking or eating at the dinner table. Next, look for salt alternatives that add flavor to your food. Herbs, spices, garlic, ginger, and even lemon juice can add enough flavors to a dish to make using salt unnecessary. Lastly, try to avoid manufactured foods.

When you first start cutting back on salt, your food might taste bland. However, you will soon find that the foods you ate before will taste unpleasantly salty. This experience is a small price to pay for the health benefits you get from lowering your salt intake.

Target iBT TOEFL Questions

1 Directions: An introductory sentence for a brief summary of the passage is provided below. Complete the summary by selecting THREE answer choices that express important ideas in the passage. Some sentences do not belong in the summary because they express ideas that are not presented in the passage or are minor ideas in the passage.

Salt consumption and blood pressure are interrelated.

-
-
-

Answer Choices

Ⓐ Blood pressure can be lowered by not taking salt.
Ⓑ High salt consumption can cause health problems.
Ⓒ Excessive salt intake is common in the United States.
Ⓓ The recommended salt intake is less than 1 teaspoon a day.
Ⓔ The problems caused by high salt intake can be solved in many ways.
Ⓕ Salt should not be used when cooking.

iBT TOEFL Vocabulary

Fill in the blanks with the appropriate words.

1 _____	**adj**	general, total, whole
2 _____	**n**	something that can be chosen instead of something else
3 _____	**adv**	in a bad or unhappy manner
4 _____	**adj**	too much, more than normal
5 _____	**v**	to spend, to use
6 _____	**v**	to achieve, to reach a goal

- overall
- excessive
- accomplish
- alternative
- consume
- unpleasantly

Human Body & Nutrition •• 125

Wrap Up

A Complete the sentences with the appropriate words.

- overall
- excessive
- accomplished
- alternative
- consume
- unpleasantly

1 The biological research team has _____ the goal in a short period time.

2 _____ sugar intake can cause health problems.

3 A little factor can have an impact on the _____ results.

4 Teens are advised to _____ enough calcium-high foods so their bones can be strong.

5 It was an _____ cold winter night.

6 There might be no _____ to solar power.

B Check (✔) the statement that is NOT mentioned as a way of reducing salt intake according to the passage <Salt and Health>.

1 Do not use salt when cooking.

2 Add flavor to a dish.

3 Avoid ready-made foods.

4 Eat more fruits and vegetables.

Practice 2

Warm Up

1 Choose three high fiber foods on the list.

☐ broccoli　　　☐ barley　　　☐ chocolate　　　☐ milk　　　☐ beans

2 Eating fiber has many benefits. How many dishes of vegetables or fruits do you consume in a day?

Read the Passage

Your time (1st): _____ min, (2nd): _____ min

The Importance of Fiber

Even though it is not a nutrient, fiber is a crucial part of our daily diet. Fiber is responsible for helping to maintain the normal functioning of our organs and our digestive tract. There are two types of fiber: insoluble fiber and soluble fiber.

A sufficient amount of insoluble fiber should be eaten each day. Insoluble fiber is found in foods such as vegetables, fruit skins and whole-wheat products. It cleans our bodies by keeping food constantly passing through. Consuming foods rich in insoluble fiber along with large quantities of water helps to ensure regular bowel movements. Additionally, the National Institutes of Health promotes the consumption of insoluble fibers because it prevents substances responsible for causing cancer from collecting in the intestines. Moreover, researchers noticed that people whose diet includes insoluble fiber tend to eat less fatty foods.

The second type of fiber is soluble fiber, which is present in certain oats and nuts. Soluble fiber lowers total cholesterol levels and is responsible for protecting our hearts.

Health experts suggest that we consume at least 20-35 grams of fiber per day. Your fiber intake should be balanced between insoluble and soluble fiber. Other basic benefits of having a high-fiber diet are that it helps our body to burn calories quicker, keeps us from overeating, increases circulation and <u>stabilizes</u> our blood sugar level throughout the day. Our overall health depends strongly upon our daily consumption of fiber.

* **stabilize:** to make steady

Target iBT TOEFL Questions

1 Directions: An introductory sentence for a brief summary of the passage is provided below. Complete the summary by selecting THREE answer choices that express important ideas in the passage. Some sentences do not belong in the summary because they express ideas that are not presented in the passage or are minor ideas in the passage.

Fiber is essential for good health.

-
-
-

Answer Choices

Ⓐ Insoluble fiber prevents diseases and obesity.
Ⓑ The National Institutes of Health suggests eating insoluble fibers.
Ⓒ Soluble fiber protects our hearts and controls cholesterol levels.
Ⓓ Soluble fibers can be found in fruits and oats.
Ⓔ A balanced intake between insoluble and soluble fiber will provide benefits to our bodies.
Ⓕ A high-fiber diet allows us not to eat much.

iBT TOEFL Vocabulary

Fill in the blanks with the appropriate words.

#		
1	**adj**	very important
2	**adv**	continually, changelessly
3	**n**	the matter of a particular kind
4	**v**	to perceive, to acknowledge
5	**n**	an advantage

- benefit
- notice
- substance
- constantly
- crucial

Wrap Up

A Complete the sentences with the appropriate words.

- crucial
- notice
- benefits
- constantly
- substances

1 Work environment is a _____ factor when choosing a company.

2 Languages are _____ evolving as people use them.

3 Winds can carry harmful _____ such as pesticides and bacteria.

4 Anyone could _____ that something is going wrong with the plan.

5 Having a good breakfast provides many _____.

B Correct the underlined parts to complete the summary note of the passage <The Importance of Fiber>.

A. Insoluble fiber
- Functions & Benefits:
  (1) keeps foods constantly passing through our digestive tract
  (2) allows <u>irregular</u> bowel movements
  (3) prevents cancer
  (4) helps people eat <u>more</u> fatty foods
- Foods: <u>meat</u>, fruit skins, whole-wheat products

B. Soluble fiber
- Functions & Benefits:
  (1) controls total cholesterol levels   (2) protects our <u>brains</u>
- Foods: oats, nuts

C. Health tips
  (1) Consume at least <u>10-35</u> grams of fiber per day.
  (2) Try to eat both insoluble and soluble fiber.

D. Other benefits of a high-fiber diet
  (1) burns calories <u>slower</u>   (2) keeps us from overeating
  (3) <u>decreases</u> circulation and stabilizes blood sugar level

Test 1

Vitamins

Vitamins are found in the food we eat every day. [■A] Vitamins help our bodies to function properly. [■B] Each vitamin plays a very specific role in the development and functioning of our bodies. They also help to process the proteins, carbohydrates and fats. Human beings use 13 different vitamins, which are divided into two categories: fat soluble and water soluble. [■C] The fat soluble vitamins are A, D, E and K, and the water soluble vitamins include all eight B vitamins along with vitamin C. [■D]

Fat soluble vitamins do not need to be used immediately and are easily stored within our bodies for up to 6 months. For example, vitamin A is largely responsible for sharpening or maintaining our eyesight and is found in foods such as carrots, citrus fruits, other orange fruits and sweet potatoes.

On the other hand, water soluble vitamins are not stored in the body and, therefore, we need to consume foods rich in such vitamins on a regular basis. For example, B vitamins create energy, red blood cells and move oxygen around the body.

When our bodies do not get enough vitamins, this is known as a deficiency. Things such as smoking, high alcohol consumption and the use of medications can hinder our bodies' ability to absorb vitamins. Deficiencies cause a great deal of harm to our bodies. Consuming a balance of foods rich in these vitamins on a regular basis is the only way to ensure that our bodies are healthy and functioning to the fullest.

1 Look at the four squares [■] that indicate where the following sentence could be added to the passage.

They also keep our immune system strong.

Where would the sentence best fit?

2 According to paragraph 1, which is true of vitamins?

  Ⓐ Each person needs different vitamins.
  Ⓑ Vitamins can be divided into 8 different categories.
  Ⓒ Vitamin A, C, D and E are fat soluble vitamins.
  Ⓓ There are 9 water soluble vitamins.

3 The word immediately in the passage is closest in meaning to

  Ⓐ temporarily
  Ⓑ carefully
  Ⓒ quickly
  Ⓓ entirely

4 The word stored in the passage is closest in meaning to

  Ⓐ saved
  Ⓑ dissolved
  Ⓒ destroyed
  Ⓓ absorbed

5 The word hinder in the passage is closet in meaning to

  Ⓐ prevent
  Ⓑ lower
  Ⓒ confirm
  Ⓓ improve

6 In paragraph 4, the author talks about the importance of vitamin intake on a regular basis by

  Ⓐ listing the advantages that vitamin intake brings to our bodies
  Ⓑ comparing the use of medications to taking vitamins
  Ⓒ explaining how a lack of vitamins can influence our bodies
  Ⓓ emphasizing how bad habits such as smoking can harm our bodies

7 Which of the following best expresses the essential information in the highlighted sentence in the passage? Incorrect answer choices change the meaning in important ways or leave out essential information.

> Consuming a balance of foods rich in these vitamins on a regular basis is the only way to ensure that our bodies are healthy and functioning to the fullest.

Ⓐ Eating vitamin-rich foods on a consistent basis is the most important factor in staying healthy.
Ⓑ Taking vitamins with a balance of foods on a daily basis can help us stay healthy.
Ⓒ People need vitamin rich foods to make their body function well and be healthy.
Ⓓ Eating vitamin-rich foods daily is the only way to prevent our bodies from operating to the fullest.

8 Directions: An introductory sentence for a brief summary of the passage is provided below. Complete the summary by selecting THREE answer choices that express important ideas in the passage. Some sentences do not belong in the summary because they express ideas that are not presented in the passage or are minor ideas in the passage.

Vitamins help our bodies operate better.

-
-
-

Answer Choices

Ⓐ We need to take vitamins every day.
Ⓑ Fat soluble vitamins are included in foods such as carrots and oranges.
Ⓒ Fat soluble vitamins can stay our bodies for around 6 months.
Ⓓ Vitamin A is essential for maintaining our eyesight.
Ⓔ Water soluble vitamins need to be taken more often since the body cannot store them.
Ⓕ Vitamin deficiency may cause health problems.

More to know — **Symptoms of Vitamin Deficiency**

- Vitamin A Deficiency: night blindness, eye dryness
- Vitamin C Deficiency: fatigue, depression, nosebleeds, swollen gums
- Vitamin D Deficiency: muscle pains, muscle weakness, bone pains
- Vitamin K Deficiency: bleeding disorder, osteoporosis

Body Clocks

Though our bodies may seem to operate out of habit, they actually follow an internal clock, which functions on a 24-hour cycle. These habit-like processes are called circadian rhythms. Our internal clocks, also called body clocks, control the temperature of our body, our sleep patterns, and hunger. It also controls the chemicals and hormones within our body.

Individual bodies have different rhythms, which means our body clocks are unique to us. This helps explain why some people are "morning people," who go to bed early, and rise early and why others are night owls, who stay awake late into the night. The rise and fall of the sun also affect our internal clocks.

[■A] Disturbing these circadian rhythms can be seriously harmful to our health and daily performance. [■B] For instance, when traveling by plane, we sometimes cross one or more time zones and feel tired or confused. [■C] Jet lag often leaves us waking up in the middle of the night or unable to sleep at night. [■D] It is related to fatigue and insomnia. If children stay awake late, their growth patterns are adversely affected and they tend to perform poorly in school. Adults are just as susceptible, too. For example, those who work at night are more likely to suffer from obesity and heart disease.

More and more, we are learning how important following our body clocks is to our health. By disrupting our sleep patterns, our bodies do not have a chance to make the necessary repairs, thus weakening our immune systems. Sleeping and eating regularly also help to create a balance within our bodies.

1 According to paragraph 1, all of the followings are controlled by our body clocks EXCEPT

Ⓐ body temperature
Ⓑ sleep patterns
Ⓒ hormones
Ⓓ heart rate

2 The word affect in the passage is closest in meaning to

　Ⓐ influence
　Ⓑ change
　Ⓒ interrupt
　Ⓓ inspire

3 The word Disturbing in the passage is closest in meaning to

　Ⓐ Beginning
　Ⓑ Confusing
　Ⓒ Balancing
　Ⓓ Operating

4 Look at the four squares [■] that indicate where the following sentence could be added to the passage.

This is called jet lag.

Where would the sentence best fit?

5 According to paragraph 3, jet lag

　Ⓐ affects growth patterns
　Ⓑ makes children stay awake late
　Ⓒ may occur when traveling across time zones
　Ⓓ is rare for adults

6 In paragraph 3, the author explains the effects on people's health when circadian rhythms are interrupted by

　Ⓐ listing the symptoms of circadian rhythms
　Ⓑ showing the causes of jet leg
　Ⓒ defining the term circadian rhythms
　Ⓓ giving some specific examples

7 **Directions**: An introductory sentence for a brief summary of the passage is provided below. Complete the summary by selecting THREE answer choices that express important ideas in the passage. Some sentences do not belong in the summary because they express ideas that are not presented in the passage or are minor ideas in the passage.

Our bodies follow an internal clock on a 24-hour cycle.

-
-
-

Answer Choices

Ⓐ Every person has different body rhythms.
Ⓑ Morning people get up earlier than night owls.
Ⓒ Children are more likely to be affected by circadian rhythms than adults.
Ⓓ People might experience health problems when circadian rhythms are disturbed.
Ⓔ Following the body clock is very important to be healthy.
Ⓕ Immune systems can be weakened if we do not sleep well.

Morning person or Night person

Why are some people early risers while others prefer to stay up late at night? Researchers have recently found a link between people's preference for mornings or evenings and a gene called Period 3. By analyzing DNA, researchers have found that people who have preference for mornings are more likely to have a long version of Period 3. In contrast, those with an extreme preference for evenings are more prone to have the shorter one.

Reading Helper

A. be responsible for ...ing

> **Examples from the passage**
>
> - Fiber **is responsible for** help**ing** to maintain the normal functioning of our organs and our digestive tract. *(The Importance of Fiber, Line 1)*
>
> - Soluble fiber lowers total cholesterol levels and **is responsible for** protect**ing** our hearts. *(The Importance of Fiber, Line 13)*
>
> - For example, vitamin A **is** largely **responsible for** sharpen**ing** or maintain**ing** our eyesight and is found in foods such as carrots, citrus fruits, other orange fruits and sweet potatoes. *(Vitamins, Line 10)*

Complete the sentences using the expressions provided in the parentheses.

1 Parents are partially responsible for _____.
(develop their child's communication skills)

2 Two factors were responsible for _____.
(destroy the environment)

3 Governments are responsible for _____.
(protect the safety of their citizens)

B. by ...ing

> **Examples from the passage**
>
> • It cleans our bodies **by** keep**ing** food constantly passing through.
>
> (The Importance of Fiber, Line 5)
>
> • **By** disrup**ting** our sleep patterns, our bodies do not have a chance to make the necessary repairs, thus weakening our immune systems.
>
> (Body Clocks, Line 19)

Complete the sentences using *by ...ing* as seen in the example.

It cleans our bodies by keeping food constantly passing through.
(keep food constantly passing through)

1 Some viruses continually adjust themselves _____.
(change their forms)

2 The company could overcome the difficulties _____.
(find the most appropriate solution)

3 The concepts can be easily understood _____.
(introduce the appropriate examples)

Actual Test

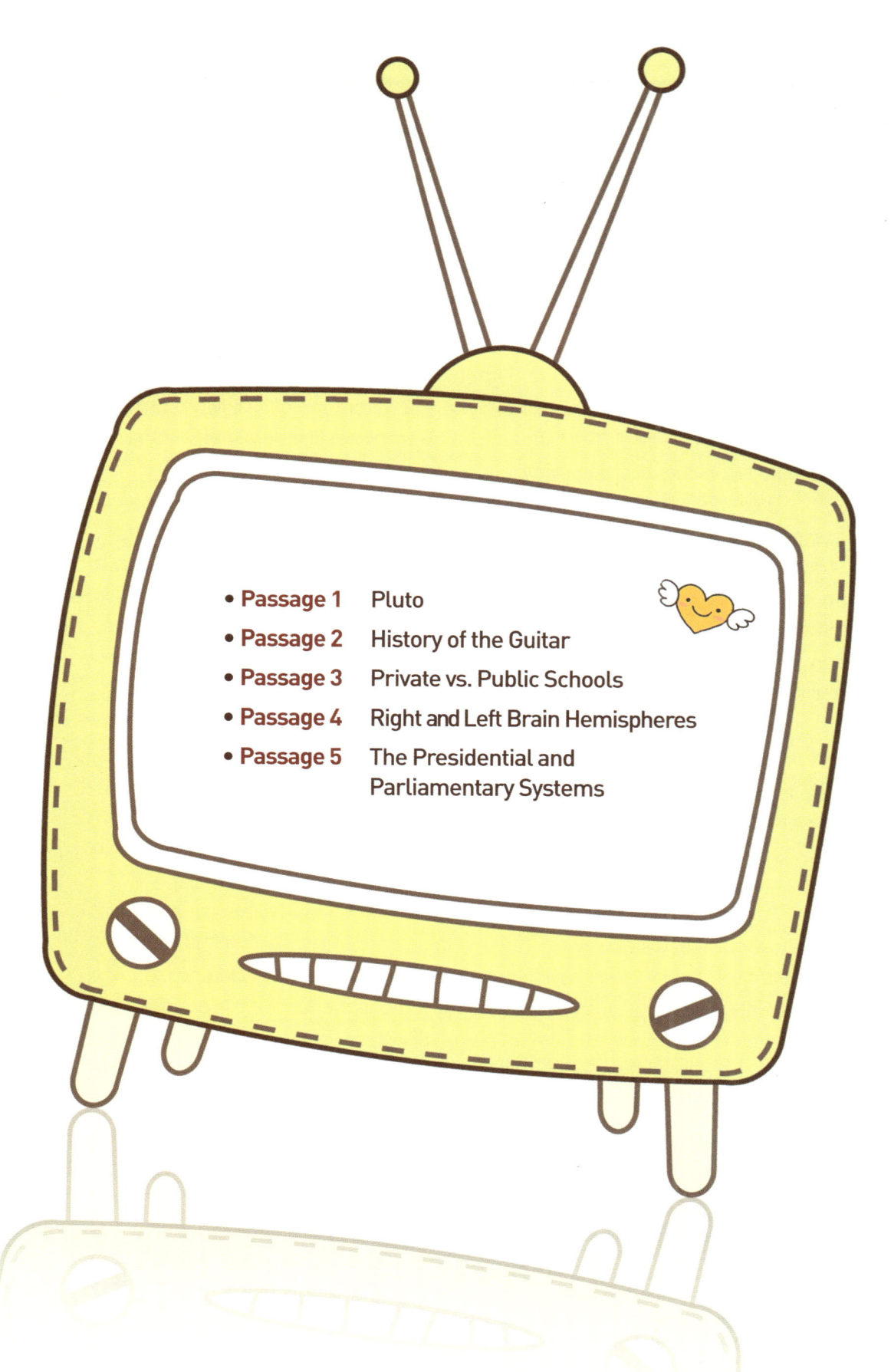

Pluto

Until recently, our solar system had nine planets: Mercury, Venus, Earth, Mars, Jupiter, Saturn, Neptune, Uranus and Pluto. However, in 2006, the International Astronomical Union removed Pluto from the official list of planets. Its name has been officially changed to a *dwarf planet*. The topic of whether or not Pluto is a planet had been very controversial since the 1930's.

There are now three criteria used to determine whether a mass in the solar system can be considered a planet. [■A] The first is that it must orbit the sun. Additionally, it also must have enough mass for gravity to compress it into a round ball-like shape. [■B] Lastly, it must have cleared other things close to its orbit out of the way. The third criterion is where Pluto does not fit. [■C] Pluto has too many other things orbiting near it and its presence has very little impact on the neighboring masses. [■D]

For many decades, Pluto remained a planet because our technology was not advanced enough to examine it and its role in the solar system. With the development of larger and more powerful telescopes, astronomers have been able to study the far ends of our solar system. Along with realizing that Pluto is not a planet, astronomers have also discovered a new class of objects that also seem to be rotating around the sun beyond Uranus and Neptune.

This re-classification of Pluto to a *dwarf planet* represents an important quality about the science field. Those in the science field believe it is critical to recognize when past ideas have been incorrect or inaccurate and to adjust them accordingly. The more scientists are willing to accept changes or correct wrong beliefs, the more we will be able to learn. This constant evolution of knowledge allows humans to benefit greatly.

* **criteria:** a plural form of criterion(a basis or standard for comparison)
* **orbit:** to circle around, to rotate

1 The word removed in the passage is closest in meaning to

   Ⓐ changed
   Ⓑ deleted
   Ⓒ selected
   Ⓓ discovered

2 Look at the four squares [■] that indicate where the following sentence could be added to the passage.

   On the contrary, the other planets have such a strong gravitational force that they control everything in their path.

   Where would the sentence best fit?

3 The word it in the passage refers to

   Ⓐ a mass
   Ⓑ solar system
   Ⓒ the sun
   Ⓓ Pluto

4 According to paragraph 2, which of the following is NOT mentioned as a criterion for planet status?

   Ⓐ The mass has to rotate around the sun.
   Ⓑ The mass should be located close to the sun.
   Ⓒ The mass must have cleared its orbital area of other objects.
   Ⓓ The mass should have sufficient mass for its self-gravity.

5 The word advanced in the passage is closest in meaning to

   Ⓐ elaborate
   Ⓑ complex
   Ⓒ widespread
   Ⓓ original

6 Which of the following best expresses the essential information in the highlighted sentence in the passage? Incorrect answer choices change the meaning in important ways or leave out essential information.

> With the development of larger and more powerful telescopes, astronomers have been able to study the far ends of our solar system.

   Ⓐ Astronomers became to be able to study more about the solar system as the telescopes appeared.
   Ⓑ The development of more advanced telescopes has allowed astronomers to study the most distant parts of our solar system.
   Ⓒ When telescopes become larger and more powerful, scientists will be able to learn more about our solar system.
   Ⓓ Telescopes have allowed astronomers to study the farthest part of our solar system.

7 According to paragraph 3, why did Pluto remain classified as a planet for many decades?
   Ⓐ Because its role was not clear.
   Ⓑ Because it rotates around the sun.
   Ⓒ Because astronomers were not interested in Pluto.
   Ⓓ Because the technology was not that advanced.

8 The word represents in the passage is closest in meaning to
   Ⓐ explains
   Ⓑ considers
   Ⓒ shows
   Ⓓ includes

9 In paragraph 4, the author discusses the importance of the constant evolution of knowledge by
   Ⓐ introducing several examples of re-classification in the science field
   Ⓑ explaining the importance of a dwarf planet in our solar system
   Ⓒ giving examples of incorrect or inaccurate ideas in the past
   Ⓓ explaining the changes that the re-classification of Pluto brings to the science field

10 **Directions**: An introductory sentence for a brief summary of the passage is provided below. Complete the summary by selecting THREE answer choices that express important ideas in the passage. Some sentences do not belong in the summary because they express ideas that are not presented in the passage or are minor ideas in the passage.

Pluto has recently been removed from the official list of planets.

-
-
-

Answer Choices

Ⓐ The amount of knowledge about our solar system will continue to grow.
Ⓑ There are Mercury, Venus, Earth, Mars, Jupiter, Saturn, Neptune, Uranus and Pluto in our solar system.
Ⓒ To be categorized as a planet, a mass in the solar system needs to meet three criteria.
Ⓓ Pluto lacks one feature to be a planet.
Ⓔ The development of technology enabled astronomers to make correction.
Ⓕ A mass in the solar system must orbit the sun.

Passage 2

History of the Guitar

The guitar is a popular musical instrument with a long history. In its typical form, the guitar features six strings, but it is sometimes manufactured with various numbers of strings. In fact, some guitars are produced with as many as 13 or 18 strings. The instrument has evolved into a device that has a wide number of uses and sounds.

The modern guitar developed from the Roman *cithara*. This instrument arrived in what is now Spain through Rome in 40 AD. By 1200 AD, the typical guitar featured four strings and was classified into two general types: the *guitarra morisca*, which had a rounded body featuring several sound holes and wide fingerboard, and the *guitarra latina*, which was similar to the modern guitar with a single sound hole and narrow neck.

Nevertheless, by the 14th century AD, the two general types were integrated, and the instrument, now known simply as the guitar, featured three pairs of strings with an extra string that played the highest note. The people of Malaga, Spain further enhanced the design by giving the instrument six single strings, and this design has remained as the most popular type of guitar for several hundred years. Not surprisingly, over such a long period of time, the guitar has been incorporated into many types of music.

[■A] In fact, the guitar is now the cornerstone of jazz, country, blues, flamenco, and rock music styles. [■B] However, it is typically adapted to each style by changing a number of features of the instrument. [■C] For example, for rock and jazz music, guitars have been modified to use electric components for sound production. In turn, the change gives artists more freedom to experiment with the instrument's sound as well as the ability to amplify it with large-scale sound reinforcement systems. [■D]

* **cornerstone:** the basic, essential, or most important part
* **amplify:** to make greater, louder

1. According to paragraph 2, which of the following is true of the Roman *cithara*?
   Ⓐ It had a narrow neck.
   Ⓑ It is the origin of the modern guitar.
   Ⓒ It came to have six strings in 1200 AD.
   Ⓓ It had several sound holes and a wide fingerboard.

2. The word integrated in the passage is closest in meaning to
   Ⓐ separated
   Ⓑ combined
   Ⓒ displayed
   Ⓓ achieved

3. The word enhanced in the passage is closest in meaning to
   Ⓐ divided
   Ⓑ changed
   Ⓒ developed
   Ⓓ offered

4. Which of the following best expresses the essential information in the highlighted sentence in the passage? Incorrect answer choices change the meaning in important ways or leave out essential information.

   Not surprisingly, over such a long period of time, the guitar has been incorporated into many types of music.

   Ⓐ The guitar and the development of music have been surprisingly interrelated for a long time.
   Ⓑ The guitar has been used to develop many different types of music for a long time.
   Ⓒ It is now wonder that the guitar has been used in many different ways in music.
   Ⓓ It is no surprise that the guitar has been used in many types of music over many years.

5. The word it in the passage refers to
   Ⓐ basis
   Ⓑ guitar
   Ⓒ instrument
   Ⓓ sound

6 Look at the four squares [■] that indicate where the following sentence could be added to the passage.

There are currently a number of genres in which the guitar has become dominant.

Where would the sentence best fit?

7 In the passage, the author explains how the guitar developed by

Ⓐ comparing the *guitarra morisca* to the *guitarra latina*
Ⓑ giving examples of various types of guitars
Ⓒ discussing the changes of the guitar over time
Ⓓ describing the changes in guitar shapes

8 Directions: An introductory sentence for a brief summary of the passage is provided below. Complete the summary by selecting THREE answer choices that express important ideas in the passage. Some sentences do not belong in the summary because they express ideas that are not presented in the passage or are minor ideas in the passage.

The guitar has a long history.

-
-
-

Answer Choices

Ⓐ The modern guitar is from the Roman *cithara* which was divided later into two types.
Ⓑ Many features of the guitar have not changed over time.
Ⓒ The instrument which finally became to have similar features to the modern guitar appeared in the 14th century.
Ⓓ The guitar has played a key role in developing many different music styles.
Ⓔ Some guitars have up to 18 strings.
Ⓕ The guitar has been used in many different music styles.

Passage 3

Private vs. Public Schools

Is a private school better than a public school at educating a child? This is not a simple question. Indeed, there are many things to consider when deciding which type of school is better suited for fulfilling a child's educational needs.

For one thing, private school students get to choose the classes that they will take. This gives each student the opportunity to study exactly what he or she is interested in, which creates an ideal learning environment. In addition, parents get to explore a wide variety of private schools and decide which one best fits their child's needs. Not to mention, even if some parents send their child to a certain private school, they can always pull the child out of the school at any time. This creates the added benefit of motivating private schools to do their best at educating children.

However, public schools are not without their merits. Public schools are full of children from the local community, so there is generally more diversity in their student populations. Because public schools have larger budgets and more students, they can offer considerably more subject options. Public schools have all of the classes that private schools offer as well as entire programs devoted to professional development, which can set up students for careers immediately after getting their diplomas.

The teachers at these institutions are another thing to consider. [■A] Private schools typically attract retired professionals who are interested in sharing their expertise with younger generations. [■B] They bring depth to the subjects they teach. [■C] On the other hand, public school teachers are experts at teaching. [■D] Before they even enter a classroom, they must undergo comprehensive teacher training and attain certifications that prove they are prepared for the job. They are particularly skilled at fulfilling the educational needs of their students and can overcome any challenges they face in the classroom.

1 Why does the author ask Is a private school better than a public school at educating a child? in paragraph 1?

  Ⓐ To emphasize that a public school is better than a private school at educating a child
  Ⓑ To question which school is better at teaching a child
  Ⓒ To introduce the main topic that is going to be discussed in the following paragraphs
  Ⓓ To show a relationship between a private school and a public school

2 The word their in the passage refers to

  Ⓐ parents
  Ⓑ private schools
  Ⓒ children
  Ⓓ public schools

3 According to paragraph 2, which of the following is mentioned as a factor that motivates private schools to do their best at teaching children?

  Ⓐ The fact that they have a small class size
  Ⓑ The fact that parents can change the school at any time
  Ⓒ The fact that there are a lot of private schools
  Ⓓ The fact that children can choose the classes

4 Which of the following best expresses the essential information in the highlighted sentence in the passage? Incorrect answer choices change the meaning in important ways or leave out essential information.

  However, public schools are not without their merits.

  Ⓐ However, public schools have no merits.
  Ⓑ Yet, public schools do not provide any advantages.
  Ⓒ However, public schools also provide benefits.
  Ⓓ In addition, the advantages of public schools are not known.

5 The word undergo in the passage is closest in meaning to

  Ⓐ understand
  Ⓑ suffer
  Ⓒ go through
  Ⓓ demand

6 The word particularly in the passage is closest in meaning to

Ⓐ exactly
Ⓑ correctly
Ⓒ extremely
Ⓓ specially

7 According to the passage, all of the following factors are used to compare a private school to a public school EXCEPT

Ⓐ facilities
Ⓑ teachers
Ⓒ programs
Ⓓ students

8 Look at the four squares [■] that indicate where the following sentence could be added to the passage.

Therefore, they can provide their students with a level of understanding that extends beyond simple theory.

Where would the sentence best fit?

9 Directions: Complete the table below about the private and public schools. Match the statements to the appropriate category. TWO of the answer choices will NOT be used.

Answer Choices

Ⓐ They offer a variety of class options.
Ⓑ Parents can have their children quit the school at any time.
Ⓒ They hire trained teachers.
Ⓓ They teach simple theory.
Ⓔ Students choose the classes that they are interested in.
Ⓕ Students can decide when to quit the schools.
Ⓖ Student populations are diverse.

Private Schools
-
-

Public Schools
-
-
-

Passage 4

Right and Left Brain Hemispheres

The human brain is a highly complex system in a human body. While being one organ, it is divided into two hemispheres. Each hemisphere has different functions and processes information in different ways. Depending on the task being performed, one hemisphere or the other is more dominant.

The left hemisphere focuses on details. It is better at logical and analytical thought. When performing structured tasks that involve various steps or when concentration on a particular part of our environment is required, the left side of the brain is used. The left side of the brain enables people to decode language to find the superficial meaning. However, the detail-oriented left hemisphere is not good at spatial perception, that is, the ability to discern the relationship between objects in view. That requires less attention to detail.

In contrast, the right hemisphere processes information on a more general level. It is the part of the brain that provides an overall view of places, things, and situations. [■A] Since the right hemisphere is the center of human imagination, people rely on this hemisphere when performing open-ended tasks requiring a creative approach. [■B] When processing language, it is the right hemisphere, which enables people to understand humor, emotion, and metaphors. [■C] Furthermore, the right hemisphere is the source of our spatial awareness. [■D]

While the above descriptions of the different functions might make it seem as if the two halves of our brain function independently of each other, most of our daily tasks are so complex that we need to use the strengths of both hemispheres in order to complete them. In terms of communication, language is a whole-brain task with the left hemisphere providing us with the literal meaning and the right brain then interpreting the context to give us a deeper, metaphorical understanding.

* decode: to understand the meaning of the words

1 The word divided in the passage is closest in meaning to

Ⓐ separated
Ⓑ retained
Ⓒ attached
Ⓓ collected

2 Which of the following best expresses the essential information in the highlighted sentence in the passage? Incorrect answer choices change the meaning in important ways or leave out essential information.

Depending on the task being performed, one hemisphere or the other is more dominant.

Ⓐ Either right or left hemisphere is more active when the task being performed is difficult.
Ⓑ Both hemispheres become activated when the task is being performed.
Ⓒ One hemisphere becomes larger according to the performance.
Ⓓ One of the hemispheres functions more actively depending on the types of task.

3 The word discern in the passage is closest in meaning to

Ⓐ show
Ⓑ support
Ⓒ understand
Ⓓ notice

4 Look at the four squares [■] that indicate where the following sentence could be added to the passage.

It enables us to analyze our environment three-dimensionally and judge distances.

Where would the sentence best fit?

5 The word them in the passage refers to

Ⓐ functions
Ⓑ daily tasks
Ⓒ strengths
Ⓓ hemispheres

6 In paragraph 4, why does the author mention communication ?

    Ⓐ To show how the human brain functions independently
    Ⓑ To explain the role of the left hemisphere
    Ⓒ To provide an example of the case which both hemispheres work together
    Ⓓ To discuss how literal meaning is understood in the right brain

7 According to paragraph 4, what can be inferred about the human brain?

    Ⓐ Two halves of human brain operate separately each other.
    Ⓑ People come to utilize both hemispheres dealing with many jobs.
    Ⓒ The right hemisphere provides people with the dictionary meaning of words.
    Ⓓ People use the right hemisphere solving detailed tasks more than often.

8 **Directions**: Complete the table below about the right and left brain hemispheres. Match the appropriate statements to the types of brain hemispheres with which they are associated. TWO of the answer choices will NOT be used.

Answer Choices

Ⓐ It is good at spatial perception.
Ⓑ It enables us to dream.
Ⓒ It is related to logical and analytical thought.
Ⓓ It becomes active when people perform open-ended tasks.
Ⓔ It enables people to speak language.
Ⓕ It is related to the ability to imagine.
Ⓖ It focuses on details.

Right Hemisphere

• _____
• _____
• _____

Left Hemisphere

• _____
• _____

Passage 5

The Presidential and Parliamentary Systems

A government controls the geographical boundaries inside which its citizens live, allowing its society to operate in an orderly fashion. When citizens manage their own government, it is known as a democracy, two of the most popular forms of which are the presidential and parliamentary systems.

The presidential system features a leader, the president, who functions as the chief executive and head of state. A president is elected through a democratic election process and operates independently of any legislative body. Nevertheless, democratic systems give an equal amount of power to the legislative bodies in order to keep a president from functioning as a dictator. In a parliamentary system, the head of state and chief executive are two separate positions. The chief executive's role is to lead the nation's legislature while the head of state fills a mainly ceremonial role.

And there are many other differences in the way the two systems function. In a parliamentary system, the chief executive, whose title is prime minister, is elected by legislature. On the other hand, the public decides who serves in this position in a presidential system. In addition, in a parliamentary system, the party members vote only along party lines. But in the presidential system, legislators are free to vote based on their own personal views. Lastly, the way that voting takes place differs as well. Legislators in a parliamentary system have a limited time to speak before voting occurs; however, presidential system legislators can delay voting by prolonging their speeches.

The parliamentary system is most common in Europe. Countries like the United Kingdom, Italy, and Spain have long established parliamentary systems, but they also exist in Asian countries like Japan and Thailand. Presidential systems are also everywhere, existing in the west in countries such as Brazil and the United States and in the east in countries like South Korea and the Philippines.

- **legislative:** relating to people who make laws
- **dictator:** a ruler who has an absolute power
- **prolong:** to lengthen in duration

1 According to paragraph 1, a democracy is when

  Ⓐ the president is elected by the public
  Ⓑ the public manages their own government
  Ⓒ the society holds two different systems
  Ⓓ the government controls its society in an orderly manner

2 The word keep in the passage is closest in meaning to

  Ⓐ hold
  Ⓑ prevent
  Ⓒ make
  Ⓓ have

3 The word separate in the passage is closest in meaning to

  Ⓐ similar
  Ⓑ different
  Ⓒ individual
  Ⓓ great

4 The word their in the passage refers to

  Ⓐ the public
  Ⓑ parliamentary systems
  Ⓒ party lines
  Ⓓ legislators

5 What is the function of paragraph 4 as it relates to the rest of the passage?

  Ⓐ It introduces European countries to describe the parliamentary system in detail.
  Ⓑ It further explains the parliamentary system in Europe.
  Ⓒ It gives examples of the countries which have the presidential and parliamentary systems.
  Ⓓ It concludes the issues discussed in the previous paragraphs.

6 Which of the following best expresses the essential information in the highlighted sentence in the passage? Incorrect answer choices change the meaning in important ways or leave out essential information.

> And there are many other differences in the way the two systems function.

   Ⓐ A lot of other differences can also be found between the operation of the two systems.
   Ⓑ Furthermore, the two systems operate in a different way.
   Ⓒ In addition, the two systems are not the same in terms of the way they function.
   Ⓓ And the two systems have a lot of differences when it comes to an election process.

7 According to paragraphs 2 and 3, which of the following is NOT true of the parliamentary system?

   Ⓐ The chief executive is elected by legislature.
   Ⓑ The party members hold the same views.
   Ⓒ The head of state and chief executive have different roles.
   Ⓓ The prime minister is elected through a democratic election.

8 Directions: Complete the table below about the presidential and parliamentary systems. Match the appropriate statements to the two types of systems with which they are associated. TWO of the answer choices will NOT be used.

Answer Choices

Ⓐ They are common in Europe.
Ⓑ The chief executive in this system is elected by legislature.
Ⓒ The president functions as a dictator in this system.
Ⓓ South Korea and the Philippines have this system.
Ⓔ This is the only form of democracy.
Ⓕ The public elects the president in this system.
Ⓖ Legislators in this system are free to vote according to their own personal views.

Presidential Systems
- _____
- _____
- _____

Parliamentary Systems
- _____
- _____

Wit&Wisdom TOEFL Series

Beginning (40~60)

The iBT TOEFL Beginner Series

★ **The iBT TOEFL Beginner**
Reading / Listening / Speaking / Writing

Perium VOCA Series

★★ **Perium VOCA for TOEFL**
Reading / Speaking / Writing

The iBT Grammar Series

★★ **The iBT Grammar**
for Beginners / for All Learners / Practice Test

Wit&Wisdom TOEFL Series

Advanced (90~110)

The iBT TOEFL Solution Series

★★★
The iBT TOEFL Solution
Reading / Listening / Speaking / Writing

The iBT TOEFL Master Series

★★★★
The iBT TOEFL Master
Reading / Listening / Speaking / Writing

PAGODA TOEFL Advanced Series

★★★★
PAGODA TOEFL Advanced
Reading / Listening / Speaking / Writing

Winning TOEFL iBT

Reading Step 3

Answer Keys

Answer Keys

Unit 1 | Education

Practice 1

Target iBT TOEFL Questions

1. Ⓐ 2. Ⓒ 3. Ⓑ 4. Ⓑ

iBT TOEFL Vocabulary

1. ambition 2. fulfill 3. mandatory
4. enroll 5. trial

Wrap Up

Ⓐ
1. mandatory 2. ambition 3. enrolled
4. trials 5. fulfill

Ⓑ
1. F 2. T 3. T
4. F 5. F

Practice 2

Target iBT TOEFL Questions

1. Ⓑ 2. Ⓒ 3. Ⓐ 4. Ⓐ

iBT TOEFL Vocabulary

1. undergo 2. pioneer 3. master
4. partially 5. restore 6. legacy

Wrap Up

Ⓐ
1. partially 2. pioneer 3. underwent
4. master 5. restored 6. legacy

Ⓑ
Helen, eye, operations, restored, 14, six, blind

Test 1 | Multiple Intelligences

1. Ⓒ 2. Ⓑ 3. Ⓑ 4. Ⓐ 5. Ⓓ
6. Ⓓ 7. Ⓒ 8. Ⓐ, Ⓒ, Ⓔ

Test 2 | Summerhill School

1. Ⓑ 2. Ⓑ 3. Ⓒ 4. Ⓐ 5. Ⓓ
6. Ⓓ 7. Ⓒ 8. Ⓓ

Reading Helper

A
1. as a world-class healthcare center
2. as a politician
3. as an inventor

B
1. the better
2. The faster
3. The clearer, the higher

Unit 2 | History

Practice 1

Target iBT TOEFL Questions

1. Ⓒ 2. Ⓒ 3. Ⓐ

iBT TOEFL Vocabulary

1. voyage 2. request 3. reach
4. convince 5. inhabitant 6. prestige

Wrap Up

Ⓐ
1. reached 2. prestige 3. inhabitants
4. voyage 5. request 6. convince

Ⓑ
1. F 2. T 3. F
4. T 5. F

Practice 2

Target iBT TOEFL Questions
1. C   2. A

iBT TOEFL Vocabulary
1. massive   2. resemble   3. respect
4. obvious   5. remarkable   6. transport

Wrap Up
A
1. resembles   2. transported   3. obvious
4. massive   5. respect   6. remarkable

B
England, tourists, bluestones, 400, worship, burial, healing

Test 1 The Great Depression
1. A   2. B   3. B   4. D   5. B
6. D   7. B   8. C

Test 2 The Silk Road
1. A   2. A   3. B   4. C   5. B
6. C   7. C

Reading Helper

A
1. **Subject:** The Italian royals, **Verb:** thought
2. **Subject:** How these stones were transported, **Verb:** remains
3. **Subject:** The sudden crash of the stock market, **Verb:** caused
4. **Subject:** The stock market's crash in October 1929, **Verb:** is referred to
5. **Subject:** The Silk Road, **Verb:** was
6. **Subject:** Indians who lived near the Ganges River, **Verb:** were
7. **Subject:** Greek sculpture techniques, this, **Verb:** gained, led to

Unit 3 | Biology

Practice 1

Target iBT TOEFL Questions
1. B   2. C

iBT TOEFL Vocabulary
1. organism   2. transplant   3. additionally
4. antibiotic   5. potential

Wrap Up
A
1. Additionally   2. antibiotic   3. potential
4. transplant   5. organism

B
plants, sun, decomposition, food, medicine, foot

Practice 2

Target iBT TOEFL Questions
1. A   2. C

iBT TOEFL Vocabulary
1. process   2. capture   3. convert
4. byproduct   5. release

Wrap Up
A
1. converted   2. process
3. release   4. captured
5. byproduct

B
sugar, light, captures, chemical, water, byproducts, Oxygen

Test 1 The Social Order of Honeybees

1. Ⓒ   2. Ⓓ   3. Ⓐ   4. Ⓑ   5. Ⓒ
6. Ⓐ   7. Ⓐ   8. Drones: Ⓐ, Ⓑ, Ⓒ
Worker bees: Ⓓ, Ⓖ

Test 2 Symbiosis

1. Ⓐ   2. Ⓐ   3. Ⓑ   4. Ⓓ   5. Ⓐ
6. Ⓒ   7. Ⓑ   8. Commensalism: Ⓑ, Ⓔ, Ⓕ   Mutualism: Ⓓ, Ⓖ

Reading Helper

A

1. Plants **differ from** all other organisms because they are able to produce their own food.
2. The sizes and formations of fungi **are different from** one type to another.

B

1. The major difference between them and other bees is that
2. Another major difference is that

Unit 4 Environment

Practice 1

Target iBT TOEFL Questions

1. Ⓑ   2. Ⓑ

iBT TOEFL Vocabulary

1. rapidly   2. extraordinary   3. finite
4. maintain 5. absolutely   6. supply

Wrap Up

A

1. supply   2. finite   3. maintain
4. absolutely 5. rapidly   6. extraordinary

B

Renewable, Non-renewable, natural gas, metal, recycling

Practice 2

Target iBT TOEFL Questions

1. Ⓑ   2. Ⓐ

iBT TOEFL Vocabulary

1. retain   2. countless   3. generate
4. productivity 5. distribute   6. disrupt

Wrap Up

A

1. generate   2. distribute   3. retained
4. productivity 5. disrupt   6. countless

B

a man-made structure used to retain water from streams or rivers, flow, urban, electricity, disrupt, construction

Test 1 Global Warming

1. Ⓒ   2. Ⓑ   3. Ⓐ   4. Ⓓ   5. Ⓐ
6. Ⓒ   7. Ⓐ   8. Ⓐ   9. Ⓐ, Ⓓ, Ⓔ

Test 2 Yellow Dust

1. Ⓒ   2. Ⓐ   3. Ⓑ   4. Ⓑ   5. Ⓒ
6. Ⓓ   7. Ⓓ   8. Ⓐ, Ⓑ, Ⓔ

Reading Helper

A

1. ②, Babies learn to speak **naturally** by being exposed to the language adults use.

2. ②, The government should react **wisely** to public opinion.
3. ②, The number of people in rural areas has decreased **significantly** over three consecutive years.

B
1. highly
2. noticeably
3. highly / noticeably / truly
4. highly / noticeably / truly
5. carefully / slowly

Unit 5 | Political Science

Practice 1

Target iBT TOEFL Questions
1. ⓒ   2. Ⓐ

iBT TOEFL Vocabulary
1. commonplace
2. prohibition
3. regulation
4. tremendous
5. accidental

Wrap Up

A
1. commonplace   2. regulation
3. tremendous   4. accidental
5. prohibition

B
1. T   2. F   3. T   4. F   5. T

Practice 2

Target iBT TOEFL Questions
1. Ⓐ   2. ⓒ

iBT TOEFL Vocabulary
1. enforce   2. dedicate   3. eliminate
4. guarantee 5. equality   6. collaborate

Wrap Up

A
1. enforce   2. equality   3. eliminated
4. collaborating   5. guaranteed
6. dedicated

B
peacekeeping, 1945, 200, improve, hunger, primary, death

Test 1 | The Beginning of Democracy
1. Ⓐ   2. ⓒ   3. ⓒ   4. Ⓑ   5. Ⓐ
6. Ⓑ   7. Ⓑ   8. Ⓓ

Test 2 | Monarchies
1. Ⓓ   2. Ⓓ   3. Ⓐ   4. ⓒ   5. Ⓑ
6. ⓒ   7. Absolute monarchy: Ⓑ, ⓒ, Ⓔ
        Constitutional monarchy: Ⓓ, Ⓖ

Reading Helper

A
1. Ⓐ
2. ⓒ
3. Ⓑ

Unit 6 | Arts

Practice 1

Target iBT TOEFL Questions
1. Ⓑ   2. Ⓖ

iBT TOEFL Vocabulary

1. largely   2. modify   3. emit
4. originally   5. incorporate

Wrap Up

A
1. largely   2. originally   3. modified
4. emits   5. incorporates

B
1. F   2. T   3. F   4. F   5. T

Practice 2

Target iBT TOEFL Questions
1. Ⓓ   2. Ⓗ

iBT TOEFL Vocabulary
1. violent   2. esteemed   3. aggression
4. recognition   5. tragic

Wrap Up
A
1. violent   2. esteemed   3. tragic
4. aggression   5. recognition

B
1. F   2. T   3. F   4. T   5. F

Test 1 The Globe Theatre
1. Ⓓ   2. Ⓓ   3. Ⓒ   4. Ⓓ   5. Ⓐ
6. Ⓐ   7. Ⓖ   8. Ⓒ

Test 2 Puppetry
1. Ⓐ   2. Ⓐ   3. Ⓑ   4. Ⓒ   5. Ⓓ
6. Ⓑ   7. Ⓓ

Reading Helper

A
1. **Though** the experiment was not successful, the researchers found important clues on the problem.
2. **Though** Mozart died at the age of 35, he composed more than 600 works.

B
1. The book is about the two soldiers' friendship **during** World War II.
2. **During** their lifetime, butterflies change their appearance several times.
3. Students can participate in many interesting programs that are provided by the community center **during** their summer vacation.

Unit 7 | Earth Science

Practice 1

Target iBT TOEFL Questions
1. Weathering: Ⓑ, Ⓓ, Ⓕ
   Erosion: Ⓒ, Ⓖ

iBT TOEFL Vocabulary
1. occurrence   2. reshape   3. extreme
4. gradual   5. dissolve   6. permanent

Wrap Up
A
1. gradual   2. dissolve   3. extreme
4. permanent   5. occurrence   6. reshaped

earthquake, erosion, wind, chemical, water, harm

Practice 2

Target iBT TOEFL Questions
1. Core: Ⓐ, Ⓔ, Ⓖ   Mantle: Ⓒ, Ⓕ

iBT TOEFL Vocabulary
1. presence   2. flourish   3. inconsistent
4. significantly   5. flexible   6. entire

Wrap Up
Ⓐ
1. flexible   2. significantly   3. presence
4. entire   5. flourish   6. inconsistent

Ⓑ
①, ②, ④, ③

Test 1   Sea Breezes & Land Breezes
1. Ⓓ   2. Ⓑ   3. Ⓐ   4. Ⓓ   5. Ⓐ
6. Ⓑ   7. Sea Breeze: Ⓑ, Ⓔ, Ⓖ
Land Breeze: Ⓒ, Ⓕ

Test 2   Clouds Types
1. Ⓒ   2. Ⓐ   3. Ⓐ   4. Ⓒ   5. Ⓐ
6. Ⓑ   7. Cirrus Clouds: Ⓒ, Ⓓ   Stratus Clouds: Ⓐ, Ⓔ, Ⓕ

Reading Helper

A

1. **Unfortunately**, the erosion humans are creating, such as deforestation and constant construction, is extremely harmful to the ecosystem. (Weathering & Erosion, Line 17)
2. **Eventually**, the warm air above the land rises and the cooler air above the sea moves inland. (Sea Breezes & Land Breezes, Line 13)

3. **Unluckily**, the erosion humans are creating, such as deforestation and constant construction, is extremely harmful to the ecosystem.
4. **At last**, the warm air above the land rises and the cooler air above the sea moves inland.

B

1. The items can also <u>be categorized by</u> their shapes and sizes.
2. The questions <u>were answered by</u> the experts.
3. The half of the electricity generated this year <u>was consumed by</u> industry.

Unit 8 | Human Body & Nutrition

Practice 1

Target iBT TOEFL Questions
1. Ⓑ, Ⓓ, Ⓔ

iBT TOEFL Vocabulary
1. overall   2. alternative
3. unpleasantly   4. excessive
5. consume   6. accomplish

Wrap Up
Ⓐ
1. accomplished   2. Excessive
3. overall   4. consume
5. unpleasantly   6. alternative

Ⓑ
4. ✔ Eat more fruits and vegetables.

Practice 2

Target iBT TOEFL Questions
1. Ⓐ, Ⓒ, Ⓔ

iBT TOEFL Vocabulary
1. crucial 2. constantly 3. substance
4. notice 5. benefit

Wrap Up
Ⓐ
1. crucial 2. constantly 3. substances
4. notice 5. benefits

Ⓑ
regular, less, vegetables, hearts, 20, quicker, increases

Test 1 Vitamins
1. Ⓑ 2. Ⓓ 3. Ⓒ 4. Ⓐ 5. Ⓐ
6. Ⓒ 7. Ⓐ 8. Ⓒ, Ⓔ, Ⓕ

Test 2 Body Clocks
1. Ⓓ 2. Ⓐ 3. Ⓑ 4. Ⓒ 5. Ⓒ
6. Ⓓ 7. Ⓐ, Ⓓ, Ⓔ

Reading Helper

A
1. Parents are partially responsible for developing their child's communication skills.
2. Two factors were responsible for destroying the environment.
3. Governments are responsible for protecting the safety of their citizens.

B
1. Some viruses continually adjust themselves by changing their forms.
2. The company could overcome the difficulties by finding the most appropriate solution.
3. The concepts can be easily understood by introducing the appropriate examples.

•• Actual Test

Passage 1 Pluto
1. Ⓑ 2. Ⓓ 3. Ⓐ 4. Ⓑ 5. Ⓐ
6. Ⓑ 7. Ⓓ 8. Ⓒ 9. Ⓓ
10. Ⓒ, Ⓓ, Ⓔ

Passage 2 History of the Guitar
1. Ⓑ 2. Ⓑ 3. Ⓒ 4. Ⓓ 5. Ⓓ
6. Ⓐ 7. Ⓒ 8. Ⓐ, Ⓒ, Ⓕ

Passage 3 Private vs. Public Schools
1. Ⓒ 2. Ⓑ 3. Ⓑ 4. Ⓒ 5. Ⓒ
6. Ⓓ 7. Ⓐ 8. Ⓒ
9. Private Schools: Ⓑ, Ⓔ Public Schools: Ⓐ, Ⓒ, Ⓖ

Passage 4 Right and Left Brain Hemispheres
1. Ⓐ 2. Ⓓ 3. Ⓓ 4. Ⓓ 5. Ⓑ
6. Ⓒ 7. Ⓑ 8. Right Hemisphere: Ⓐ, Ⓓ, Ⓕ Left Hemisphere: Ⓒ, Ⓖ

Passage 5 The Presidential and Parliamentary Systems
1. Ⓑ 2. Ⓑ 3. Ⓑ 4. Ⓓ 5. Ⓒ
6. Ⓐ 7. Ⓓ 8. Presidential Systems: Ⓓ, Ⓕ, Ⓖ Parliamentary Systems: Ⓐ, Ⓑ

Winning TOEFL is a three-step series for beginning level students who are preparing for iBT TOEFL. Each step consists of four books: Listening, Reading, Speaking and Writing.

Winning TOEFL will help students be familiar with iBT TOEFL question types and provide opportunities to develop essential test skills through a step-by-step process.

Key Features of Winning TOEFL Reading
- Focused practice for each question type
- Step-by-step practice for the development of test skills
- TOEFL passages on important academic topics
- Essential TOEFL vocabulary
- Full answer keys